The Art of Valuation

The Art of Valuation

Edited by
Arlo Woolery
Lincoln Institute of Land Policy

Lexington Books
D.C. Heath and Company
Lexington, Massachusetts
Toronto

Library of Congress Cataloging in Publication Data

Main entry under title:

The Art of valuation.

   Transcript of 2 panel conversations held in Cambridge, Mass., summer, 1977, featuring J.C. Bonbright, J.W. Martin, and R.B. Welch.
    1. Public utilities—United States—Valuation—Congress.   2. Public utilities—Taxation—United States—Congress. I. Woolery, Arlo. III. Bonbright, James Cummings, 1891–   II. Martin, James Walter, 1893–
IV. Welch, Ronald Burton.
HD2765.A77   338.4'3   78-5471
ISBN 0-669-02340-X

Published simultaneously in Canada

Printed in the United States of America

International Standard Book Number: 0-669-02340-X

Library of Congress Catalog Card Number: 78-5471

Contents

Preface

Conversation is like a meandering stream, seldom flowing in straight lines and seldom contained within well-defined banks. Conversations characteristically are strewn with nonsequiturs whose number increases with the number of participants. When more than a dozen eager participants are brought together for two full days of animated conversation, it is inevitable that some explore different tributaries of the main stream, which thus leads to some twists and turns that are totally unexpected, and there may be occasions when the readers suddenly find themselves on the opposite bank of the stream with no recollection of ever having crossed a bridge. They should assume that the stream has suddenly changed directions, and I hope they are capable of accepting surprise as an experience to be enjoyed as a vicarious participant in the conversations. We would live in a poor world, indeed, if it provided us with no surprises. So the readers are urged to make adjustments to abrupt changes with good humor and the full realization that their companions in conversation also may have found themselves in many places that were not their original destinations.

Throughout this transcript, footnotes have been kept to a minimum because conversation tends to incorporate footnote information within itself. Also, footnotes would to a certain extent be after the fact and to a certain extent a third-party intrusion. The few footnotes included fall into two distinct categories. The first is that of explaining items that are assumed to be well known to all of the actual participants in this conversation. The second category pertains to various pieces of litigation discussed in the conversation and subsequently decided in court.

I am indebted to Mary O'Brien, Lincoln Institute of Land Policy Librarian, for her help in making necessary corrections to the original transcript of the taped conversations. Also my debt extends to Sharon Byrd, Annelies Fulscher, and Nancy Cook for their good natured typing and retyping of the various drafts of the manuscript. It is impossible to find a proper way of expressing thanks to James C. Bonbright, James W. Martin, and Ronald B. Welch for coming to Cambridge in the heat of summer and spending two days to allow neophyte valuers to draw so heavily on their collective experience in the field of railroad and utility valuations. Last but far from least, special thanks should go to Clyde Reeves for his assistance in coordinating the entire program and serving as moderator for our two days of stimulating conversation.

Arlo Woolery

List of Panelists

C. Lowell Harriss
> Professor of Economics, Columbia University
> Associate, Lincoln Institute of Land Policy, Bronxville, New York

Robert McSwain
> Director, Franchise Tax Division, Alabama Department of Revenue
> Faculty Advisory Committee, Lincoln Institute of Land Policy, Montgomery, Alabama

Charles McCreath
> Utility Appraiser, Idaho State Tax Commission, Boise, Idaho

Gerald McDougall
> Professor, College of Business Administration, Wichita State University, Wichita, Kansas

Kenneth Morrison
> Property Assessment Division, Montana Department of Revenue, Helena, Montana

James O'Brien
> State Assessed Property Section, Minnesota Department of Revenue, St. Paul, Minnesota

Oliver Oldman
> Learned Hand Professor of Law and Director of the International Tax Program, Harvard Law School, Cambridge, Massachusetts
> Faculty Advisory Committee, Lincoln Institute of Land Policy, Cambridge, Massachusetts

Bruce Taylor
> Independent Appraiser, Bradford, Vermont
> Formerly with Vermont Department of Revenue

Arlo Woolery
> Executive Director, Lincoln Institute of Land Policy, Cambridge, Massachusetts

Conversations

First Day

A conversation with three valuers—James C. Bonbright, James W. Martin, and Ronald Welch, each commending the vocation but not his own specific conclusions about it.

Reeves: Good morning to you, gentlemen. I have the pleasure of welcoming you on behalf of those workers in valuation seated around this table. We hope that we may have the benefit of your counsel on matters of value and valuation this fresh July morning. The valuation science—or art, if you so choose—owes more to you three gentlemen than any other collective trio of people. Many of us have for the past forty years been putting your old wine in new bottles and have found it to be of excellent vintage. However, it now seems appropriate that we begin the training of some new vintners, and they have come here to seek the guidance of you who have developed so much of the theory and practice that has become the daily tools of our trade. We hope to obtain from you guidance as to the directions we should be pursuing in the future, because if there is one thing we have learned, it is that there is nothing as permanent as change, and it may well be that we have not caught up with the great changes that have taken place over the past half of a century. These changes are coming at an accelerating rate so that we are finding, like Alice, we must run faster and faster just to stay where we are. It would be most helpful for us if you three gentlemen who have done so much in the past would do one more thing, and that is to indicate some parts of the valuation vineyard that may need future cultivation and perhaps also to point out nooks and crannies that may have in the past been overlooked, but still show potential for yielding good fruit. I have told Professor Bonbright that I and many others in the valuation field have been reading his treatise nearly all of our lives, and I guess that is one reason why his work is referred to in valuation areas as the "bible"—because even though you spend a great deal of time in reading and rereading, you never seem to finish it. Nobody ever sits down and reads the bible through from cover to cover. Decades ago many gave up on the property tax, and now it is probably more viable than it ever was. Unfortunately, assessment rates and tax burdens seem to have increased much more rapidly than the body of knowledge and methodology behind getting the job done. The theory indeed has far outpaced the practice. But now, we are confronted with a situation that draws heavily on existing knowledge and requires a generous infusion of new thought. In the assessment of public service-type corporations, it seems as if the theory is not as good as it used to be—or the input to the model that you construct to bring about these assessments has become a lot different than it used to be. There are really two areas in the assessment field that appear to me as being ones in which we might undergo considerable progress in the next number of years. One would be the application of computer technology in mass appraisals. The Lincoln Institute of Land Policy and a number of other organizations are working on this, and I think a great deal of progress is being made and will continue to be shown. So, that particular aspect of the problem will come up for relatively little discussion here today because it involves a kind of technology and procedure that is alien to many of us. The other area, which we are hopefully going into in considerable depth, is that of valuing public service-type corporations for ad valorem tax purposes. I do hope that through some kind of a miracle, we might come out of this meeting with the feeling that we have made the beginning of renewed interest in the complex problems surrounding the valuation and taxation of railroad and utility properties. Perhaps we can also point the way and provide some encouragement for new and continuing scholarship that might rival or, in my most optimistic flights of fancy, exceed even that of Bonbright, Martin, and Welch. Dr. Bonbright was in this field "the first with the most," and I am going to invite him to touch off this discussion with some background of how a man in the 1920s and 1930s could possibly have been provoked to work as long and as hard as he did to produce the bible on valuation problems.[a] Would you respond to that, Professor Bonbright?

Defining Value

Bonbright: Yes, that's a good question. It was asked me once by my dear friend, Professor Robert L. Hale, who was a specialist in public utilities and public utility valuation. But he put it in other words. He said, "James, why did you waste your time on all of that business about valuation and value when no one knows what those words really mean?" He said, "You might as well have written a book about the meaning of *cat*—an animal—or *cat*—the first syllable of catamaran—or *cat*—the first syllable of catastrophe." He said, "This is simply writing about a word that really has a multiple of meanings." There is something in what he said. However, I'd gone so far that I could not stop in spite of all of his forebodings. What really brought me into the field was my special interest in the economics of the public utility industry and more especially in public utility rate regulation. I was much impressed with the trouble that commissions and courts at that time had when they undertook to distinguish the "fair value" used for other legal purposes such as taxation.

This gave rise to at least two different meanings of "value" where public utility property was concerned. The first was value for rate regulation and the second was value for taxation. But after looking at some of the tax and rate cases, I came to the conclusion that there are not just two meanings of "value,"

---

[a]Bonbright, James C., *The Valuation of Property*, 2 vols. (Charlottesville, N.C.: The Michie Company, 1937; 1965 reprint). See Appendix A.

but there are many meanings to this most elusive word and concept and that they might possibly be worth investigating together because most of them are interrelated—because there is no cat as an animal and cat as the first syllable in catamaran. Anyway, it just happened to be the right time for this study at Columbia University because it was the kind of work that could be undertaken only by a fairly large number of staff members. We were then in the midst of the awful depression of the 1930s, and as a result, it was possible to engage a fair number of graduates from the law school as well as many students who were looking for something to occupy their time and provide the small amount of income necessary to maintain their livelihoods. The result was that more than twenty people were brought into the effort, and they in turn had a great deal of help from various conferences and from communications with other experts in the field.

The project was financed by the Columbia University Council for Research in the Social Sciences, which Professor Frederick C. Mills and I had organized two or three years before, although we had not yet thought of this particular use of the funds, which came mostly from the Rockefeller Foundation.

The essence of the book is that words have many meanings and that *value* is a word of more meanings than most words. As Justice Holmes said, "A word is not a crystal, transparent and unchanged; it is the skin of a living thought, and may vary greatly in color and content according to the circumstances and the time in which it is used."

Our volumes were really an attempt by us to distinguish among the various meanings of the word *value* and also to determine the interrelationship between *value* and the *evidences of value*, among other things. I recall the late Percy Bridgeman of the Harvard Physics Department saying that the accepted evidence gives the very meaning of a term, such as *length* in physics. It is not a particular way of measuring length that determines what it is. The evidence is the length. If you explain how to measure length, you have already defined what length means. Any other attempt of definition is in vain—meaningless. If we were to work on a new edition of the book, we might spend some more time trying to determine how *value* ought to be defined. However, at the time we did our work, we did not have the benefit of Percy Bridgeman's incisive thinking on measurement contained in his volume, *Logic of Modern Physics*.

What I would like to talk about next is a problem that has intrigued me for a long time, and that is the problem of the valuation of a part of an organic whole. This is the kind of problem that is faced by a state like New Jersey when it sets about to determine the value of a railroad that runs through New Jersey, New York, and Pennsylvania. It is interesting that there was no disagreement among the twenty-odd staff members about the approach to this particular problem. They felt that it was necessary to start by distinguishing two primary and rather basic definitions, or concepts, of "value." And that was simply the distinction between market value in the general sense of the price at which the property can be sold and value to the owner. This latter value is the value that the owner would attach to his property as measured by the loss he would suffer if he were to be deprived of the use and the ownership of that property. These two values can be distinguished in their extreme form by the illustration of the left-hand member of a pair of gloves. As far as I know, there is no market for single left-hand or single right-hand gloves. Hence, the market value of a left-hand glove alone, or of a right-hand glove, is zero. They really can't be sold for anything. On the other hand, if a person loses his left-hand glove, his entire set of gloves, which may have been worth $7 to begin with, becomes worthless. So, on one hand in that extreme case, the market value of the property, the left-hand glove, is zero; but the value to the owner is $7 or the entire value of the set of gloves.

Well, what practical bearing does the example just stated have on the allocation of taxable valuation to various states or various districts within a state? What bearing does it have on the tax problem of allocating shares of the whole value to any specific district? It is simply this: One must give up the idea of a reasonable allocation of the value of a railroad running through New Jersey, New York, and Pennsylvania. Actually, a reasonable allocation of value to the state of New Jersey cannot be properly regarded as an attempt to find out what the New Jersey portion of the property is worth and to say what its value was is simply to beg the whole question of valuation. Our problem is that of finding a reasonable allocation of value, and we must make it reasonable, not because it is defining a value of the New Jersey portion, but it has to be reasonable for some other reason. Aside from obvious choices of this versus that proposed method of valuation—miles of track, rough estimates of reproduction cost, with or without depreciation—aside from highly practical but very important considerations such as the expense of making a particular value relation, we must be concerned with what legislators and judges may do. They may think that what you are trying to do is find the value, and they will continue to think so even though it is not true. Aside from that, the only thing that I can think of that would make this allocation rather than that allocation more desirable is to turn back to the purpose or purposes of the particular tax and ask yourself why do you value a $50 million property any more than a $5 million property. And why do you tax it more. A very brief scanning of some of the literature on taxation seems to suggest two possible answers, one being that the owner of a $50 million property is a richer man than the owner of a $5 million property. The ability to pay principle would be invoked as the argument in favor of higher taxes for the owner of the $50 million property.

The second possibility is that the benefit received by the owner of the more expensive property is greater and therefore he should pay a greater amount of taxes. And if we examine the question entirely from the cost point of view, the government cost of serving the $50 million property may be ten times greater than the corresponding cost for serving the $5 million property. And therefore, the proper allocation aside from the many practical problems with feasibility of determination should be decided at least in part by reference to these three criteria—that is, these are the three reasons for taxing the more valuable property at a higher amount. But I keep coming back to the conclusion of the book that finds that any attempt to apportion or allocate the property of a railroad located in various states to any individual state by trying to determine what the value in the individual state happens to be is in vain. It is an almost meaningless exercise. The value of the property within an individual state is not what you are or should be after, although you may have to pretend that is your goal. It is not what you are really seeking, even though the courts may say that they think that is what you are after and may even overrule you if you do not say it.

Reeves: I must say this has been a most interesting and challenging dissertation on the many problems involved in valuation and allocation. I must confess you left me feeling just a little bit vague about what we are really after in this whole field cf valuation and allocation of the property values of utility industries.

Bonbright: That's what I was trying to do.

Reeves: I tried to leave taxpayers with this feeling more than once, but I find they do not laugh that way.

Oldman: I would like to pose this question for Professor Bonbright. I certainly enjoyed the presentation and am delighted after all the years of reading his two fine volumes on valuation of property to find out exactly how the entire work originated. But to get to my question—in using your example of the meaninglessness of asking about the value of the railroad property in New Jersey, I am not sure whether you carefully avoided the parallel question about what is the value of the railroad property in all of the three states mentioned. I would like to have you address yourself to the problem of valuing the total railroad property in New Jersey, New York, and Pennsylvania without any question of dividing it up; or, for the moment, let us assume that the railroad property is in a single jurisdiction and address ourselves to the problem of determining its value. I take it that this would not be a meaningless question.

Bonbright: No, not meaningless. But, of course, there are problems in valuing the entire railroad property. I suppose one of the first questions if you are doing valuation for the property tax is to address yourself to the question of how much of the railroad is property—that is, how much of the railroad is really rail property that belongs in the legally defined tax base.

Oldman: Well that, of course, is the central theme of your book. We must continually be asking ourselves why we are making the valuation in question.

That question will surface whether you're valuing a railroad or any other kind of property. In both valuation and allocation problems, you are always asking yourself that question in the general sense as soon as you ask the abstract question: "What is the value?" If you ever ask the abstract question about any piece of property—what is its value—that must be a meaningless question. I am not sure whether you meant to say that.

Bonbright: I think it is a meaningless question unless behind it is some assumed concept of value that gives it meaning. But you may not have to state that assumption in words because you are talking with people who in general have the same perception of value that you have.

Oldman: But, if we just make the one assumption that you made at the beginning as to the two basically different types of value—that is, market value in the sense that the property would be bought and sold with price indicating value, or that all property has a certain value to the existing owner and that value is measured by the loss the owner would suffer if he were deprived of the property—then we can continue saying that the market value of railroad property in New Jersey does not constitute the basis for a useful investigation. It might be useful, though, to investigate the market value of the whole railroad property initially as if it were in a single jurisdiction. There, you do have some concept of value in mind, and that is market value.

Bonbright: I am not quite sure what you have in mind, but it may be that you can find the market value of the New Jersey property by using the market value of New York and Pennsylvania property and then apportioning some of the total value on the basis of existing relationships. Actually, of course, if you try to find the value of the New York property, the New Jersey property, and the Pennsylvania property and add them all together, you call the result market value, and the result is only market value because you made the sum of the parts add up to equal the whole.

Now an interesting question arises. When you do have this market value as a whole and you begin prorating on ratios other than those determining the original values of the parts, you may be allocating an amount of value that was different from the original value of the parts. And this comes about because we do not have any real evidences of the true value of the part that lies within any one of the states that we have mentioned. Obviously, the cost of the New Jersey railroad is a meaningless concept. Your income is indivisible among the portions arising in the various states; you have no market and no sales for the parts of the property. You can get a meaningful estimate of the value of the entire property, but no meaningful estimate of the value of its parts, which is what I really started off to say at the beginning of my discussion. And, of course, this is where I really started off—to see whether you were solving the prime problem of making a distinction between the value of the whole and the value of the sum of the individual parts.

It occurs to me that when you are valuing a railroad property in the whole for property tax purposes, you are not really valuing it in the whole to begin with because this is a property tax and the property tax does not identify the railroad as a whole—that is, it is not a tax against the entire interstate railroad system. Also, there is the further problem of breaking down the value of the company to the operating property of the railroad that is being taxed. We would not want to include the oil lands owned by Union Pacific in the tax base of the operating railroad property. So, even though some of the assets of the railroad are called railroad company assets, they are not taxable as part of the railroad operating property. You cannot start with the value of the whole without making some kind of apportionment or allocation between the value of the big whole and the value of that part of the whole that you regard as a whole for property tax purposes.

Oldman: Certainly you are quite right. If we are talking only about the property tax, then we must have before us some concept of property within the meaning of the base that you regard as a tax base, and some of the total value of the railroad goes well beyond the meaning of property unless it is specifically subject to taxation. So, right away you have a different type of allocation problem, partly between intangible and tangible property, but partly also, as you point out, you may have assets owned by the company that are out of the jurisdiction of the three states we were talking about and also nonrailway property like the oil wells. These out-of-state aspects are pretty easy to eliminate. The values of the tangible and intangible property may be very difficult to separate out, especially if the only value evidence is income data. I gather that this difficulty is really at the heart of a lot of the problems of utility and railroad valuation. But that does not mean you should not try to do it.

Bonbright: Well, there are many criticisms of the property tax for railroad property, and a good many railroad spokesmen and economists have advocated some form of taxation that would put railroad property on more or less the same basis as their various competitors.

Oldman: The problem with that is that it is much more than just a foot in the door. Almost any property owner who has to pay property taxes can come up with a very effective argument as to why we ought to eliminate the application of the property tax to his particular property. He can always say that we should devise some other way of taxing his particular property. And I cannot think of any kind of property for which we cannot make a respectable argument on this score. The real difficulty here is that if you have a tax that is the backbone of most local government revenues, then there just is not any real substitute for the property tax. I think I have heard Lowell Harriss say this a large number of times. So, it is my feeling that we can take the property tax as given and assume there is no real substitute for it for supporting the needs of local government. The question then becomes what do you do about railroads if you have a property tax?

Bonbright: I guess that anyone who thinks rationally can put up a perfectly good reason as to why he should not be taxed under the method currently in question.

Reeves: Since we have reached this point in our discussion about railroad property, I think it would be nice to hear from Professor Martin since he has been struggling with this problem for well over forty years and continues to do so. In fact, he has been involved quite recently in some very substantial investigations into the valuation problems surrounding railroad property. So perhaps this would be a good time to let Professor Martin state the problem as he sees it from his particular vantage point.

Capitalized Earnings

Martin: It seems to me that matters of profound importance have been raised here when it was said that you must depend upon capitalization of income to determine value for the operating property of the railroad industry. Let me re-phrase that, however. I use the term *income* very loosely. As Thomas S. Adams says, under certain circumstances that may mean gross receipts from the operation of the railroad, and under different circumstances, certain other income measures may be used. I would like to refer to gross receipts not as income but as total revenue or gross revenue. There are numerous other measures of income that can be used, just as there are numerous measures of income that are used for estimating our gross national income. I guess the U.S. Department of Commerce has three or four or five different measures. In addition to them, you have a number of others that are officially used in the United States when you are talking about the income of the people of a state or a county or the whole country or whatever size of political jurisdiction.

I would like to start out by suggesting a hypothesis and not a conclusion. One must make a distinction between a conclusion and an hypothesis. The hypothesis is that we have at the present time, or we will have soon, no other means of making estimates of the value of railroads or the unit value of railroad property except capitalization of some major earnings indicator. I pose this hypothesis with a certain measure of regret because I feel that it is unfortunate from the point of view of valuation people because it does increase the work involved and in all probability it will decrease the precision of the end product.

So I will make this not quite as a prediction but as some thing that will move our discussion along more effectively than if we do not make the assumption, or perhaps I should continue to say "accept the hypothesis." So let's set that up as one of the things that we must deal with.

For the moment, I would like to focus on the cause. When I first began the job of tax valuation of railroads, we had about ninety companies as I remember. For most of these, we could get satisfactorily quoted values of stock. For 1974 and 1975, I have tried to do similar valuations, and I can find corresponding data on only eight railroads. Now other classes of corporations are going the same route, but I believe railroad companies are getting there faster than any other category unless it be the trucking industry. I must not dwell overly long on trying to make the point that the stock-and-debt method of valuation is rapidly becoming a thing of only historical importance, but is no longer effective as a major valuation tool.

The second thought I have is that the major deficiencies in the cost approach of estimating value have made it meaningless for general application. And if this already had not been so, the extraordinary price revolution that has occurred in recent years certainly has finished the job. Of course, it had been my feeling that the cost approach as a method of estimating value had been finished many years ago. It has taken longer to persuade some of my colleagues, but I now think that even the most steadfast of them feel that the cost approach to valuation has, at most, very limited value. It is my opinion that if you look at the thing without reaching your conclusion before you start the valuation process, there is no way in which you can use it, at least in general application.

Now that does not say you cannot use cost. You can use cost, and you must use cost in some particular applications. The best and most pervasive illustration that I think will stand up for the time being is that of making adjustments for additions of assets to the public service property during a given year. You can use the cost basis for making that estimate because it constitutes a series of transactions that occur during a given year, and estimating obsolescence is not a major problem. Also, the additional assets are generally a small fraction of the total value of the property, and this also reduces the magnitude of error. There are numerous other specific applications, but each is of rather limited scope. But as far as general application of the cost approach is concerned, it seems to me that it is a "gone gosling." These are the reasons that I ask you to accept with me the hypothesis that we either now have or shortly will have no alternative to capitalization of earnings as a method of valuation.

Now, that suggests very strongly that one of the problems that confronts us today is to improve our means of using capitalization of earnings. In other words, how do we determine the earnings of railroads, how do we define them, how do we work with them to come up with meaningful figures that we can use in this capitalization process? I personally think that we must become more innovative in our methods of approach to the valuation of railroad and interstate pipeline properties. I am attacking some of the current problems with some things that I hope will shed at least a few rays of new light on this particular problem. We have been having to abandon things that we never thought we would abandon, and I think we are going to wind up abandoning a lot more if we are really going to improve things in the valuation field. We may be limited to using the earnings approach in estimating the unit value that Mr. Bonbright has spoken about so well. Although he may have understressed the earnings basis for estimating value by perhaps overstressing the allocation problems that follow once you have estimated the value of the unit, I should mention that I am not lacking accord with his general viewpoint. I agree entirely with the viewpoint that he expressed. The only trouble I see is that the tools with which to do it are not readily at hand, and I do not think we know many of the answers. So I would like to advance a few suggestions that may help in tackling this problem and finding some answers for it. And, I should add, that is exactly what I am doing with some work at home in Kentucky. I am tackling this problem and trying to find some answers, and to date I have found more bad answers than good answers.

Let me point out some of the problems facing practical valuation people who know many of the key facts involved. One of the key facts, of course, is the decline in the number of corporations of particular classes for which you can get good quotations on selling prices of shares of stock. You can make estimates of bond values, but you cannot make estimates of stock values that are truly defensible. Here I should mention that I am talking about common stock. Rarely can you make accurate estimates of preferred stock, although sometimes it is possible. That is only one problem.

Another problem is that a very, very large proportion of all of the public utility corporations have been reorganized in some form. In some categories—that is, some classes of public utilities—the organization moves have gone way beyond what any of us envisioned a few years ago.

Thirdly, in recent years, to a remarkable extent that we would never have anticipated in the 1940s or early 1950s, the corporations engaged in the public service businesses are now engaged in a whole range of other businesses, and this produces another allocation problem. In other words, you have to do some kind of an allocation to get rid of that part of the business that the corporation conducts that is not public service—not railroad service, not electric power service, not any kind of a public utility operation. This is an old problem, and the first paper I wrote on this problem was published in the *Journal of Land and Utility Economics* in 1940. So, this is not a new issue, but it is of extraordinary importance now as compared with the situation previously.

Now this difference is related to some other occurrences that constitute for us a major disaster, and the extent to which it is truly major depends first of all on the agreement with the hypothesis that I suggested at the outset and, second, on one's choice of attack on the capitalization rate problem. But, in any case, we have a collection of changes that bring about changes in the balance sheet and the income statement. These changes in the public service corporation reports are simply devastating in their effect on how you employ the capitalization of earnings for estimating value. Now one of those, which derives from the federal income tax laws as first passed in the early 1960s and later amended in the early 1970s and again amended recently, on the one hand, involves certain deferments of federal income tax liability of corporations and, on the other, sets up an investment credit that reduces the current tax liability. I may be skipping a lot of the technicalities involved, but these are two of the major elements in explaining what this whole business has done to me and has done to the balance sheet and to the income statement as well. Now today when you deal with a measure of income, do you deal with it exactly as shown on the income statement from the public service corporation, or do you have to modify that income statement in order for it to make any sense in the valuation process? One of the reasons for that question is this: Do you count that accrual for what the Interstate Commerce Commission calls "provision for deferred taxes" as a current item or do you not? Now I am not married to any answer to this question, and I am not married to any answer on any other aspect of this whole business. I would like to make this point clear, and I am sure that my colleagues know that.

There are some people who have referred to Martin as an advocate of the capitalization of gross receipts. That never was true of me, and I can assure you it is not true today. I did use the capitalization of gross receipts at one time. That was when I tested it and found it to be a better indicator of value than other levels of the income stream that were available to me, and so I used the best thing that I could find under the circumstances. But I did not advocate the use of gross receipts to the exclusion of other measures of earnings. However, I did find it helpful during part of the 1950s when the upset in measures of earnings was considerable.

I think the number one reason for this upset was the excess profits tax. This particular provision of our tax law did cause problems while it was in operation, and even after it was discontinued, there were still numerous suits pending in court that made its effects felt. This was one major reason for using capitalized gross earnings as an indicator of value during this particular time period. However, there were other reasons in the existing economic picture that made gross receipts a better indicator of capital value of public service property than other more generally accepted measures of earnings.

Oldman: Mr. Martin, may I ask you two questions on what you were just saying? One relates to the valuation of the public service companies you were just speaking about. Was this valuation done in connection with the property tax or for rate-making purposes?

Martin: For property tax purposes, I do not have any truck with the rate base. My friend Mr. Bonbright is the rate base expert; I am not.

Oldman: Well, he is really an all-purpose expert.

Martin: Yes, sir, but I am talking about general valuation where we are really trying to find market value figures.

Oldman: But in the property tax context, I assume?

Martin: Yes, most of these valuations were in the property tax context. However, others were for borrowing programs, some were for sales purposes, and some for condemnation purposes.

Oldman: You are not arguing that you would use the same value for all of these purposes that you have listed, are you?

Martin: Yes, but with reservations. Of course, as you know much better than I, different states have different legal restrictions on, just for example, the valuation for condemnation. I did a chore in Missouri some years ago in which I had to get instructed in the rules of the game for condemnation all over again. So the answer is yes, but not for 100 percent of the cases. And also, by the way, not for 100 percent of what we call market value, and that holds true for the property tax also. You have to do some maneuvering, depending upon a state law to actually deal with valuation for property tax purposes also. You have already raised some questions that seem to bear on that issue. You have also left some elements hanging.

Oldman: I wanted to ask a related question, and I should point out that this question is asked by somebody who has not been studying valuation of public utilities for property tax purposes. I have to stay away from that in my course work and regard it as just too specialized a field now to get my students involved in. But I have always been curious about it, and I wanted to learn more. So, I approach any question that I am asking here from the point of view of ignorance rather than from having read a lot of cases. But the question that I really wanted to ask is this: You pointed out earlier that at least at one point you found that capitalized gross earnings was a better or preferred approach to use for estimating value than capitalizing net income?

Martin: Preferred in a sense that it was a function of the total value of operating property in the cases where you had total value. We used sales where sales data were actually available, and I should point out that sales data are really very limited for this type of property. So, we used a combination of sales data where available and the stock-and-debt indicator of value and found that the relationship between gross receipts and selling price and stock-and-debt indicators of value was closer during part of the 1950s than the correlation between net railway operating income and sales data or stock-and-debt indicators of value. And this especially was true, and still is, of railroad properties.

Oldman: But that assumes that you know the answer before you actually start.

Martin: No, it does not. You apply statistical measures specifically in the area of coefficients of correlation and dispersion. Relationships are determined on the basis of transaction data. For railroad property, the financial trade area, not the property to be valued for tax purposes, was the basis.

Oldman: But doesn't that assume that such information as you had from stock-and-debt indicators was good information. Earlier in the discussion, I think, it was mentioned that the stock-and-debt method would have been a terrible basis for estimating value, so I am finding it difficult to identify the criterion that enables you to choose capitalized gross earnings as being more closely correlated with value than capitalized net railway operating income. My question is only what is the criterion and I guess your answer is the stock-and-debt method.

Martin: No, sir, not quite but almost. "Almost" because there really was not any other method available for estimating value. One point I would like to make for that purpose is this: The stock-and-debt method of estimating value is a really reliable basis, and I believe I can support this contention statistically also. It is very helpful for making a valuation of any one individual corporation's holdings of a public service company. Developments in the recent past render the stock-and-debt basis of estimation for any use less and less reliable.

Oldman: You mean an average of stock and debt?

Martin: That's right, and the reason, of course, is the common one that there are compensating elements—what one method lops off, the other one picks up.

Oldman: The analogy to that is saying that the market for ordinary real estate—that is, the prices in the transactions—constitute your best guide as to the value of the property. What you are saying is that in the utility area, the analogy for that market is the market value as indicated by the stock-and-debt method. And, if it is an active market, then that ought to be a criterion.

Martin: Yes, but with this reservation. In certain particular classes we identified a considerable number of sales for the particular year in which we made valuations. It is extremely difficult to use information that you can gather through the financial press and otherwise. But we do include this information along with other information about the parties to the sale and so on. And we also discuss this information with the tax officials in the individual state. However, there were very few areas where the sales provided usable data. If I remember correctly, the two major classes that we could use were truck lines and gas pipelines. There were verifiable sales for these particular property classes. I think these were the only two classes where we found enough sales to make any use of and I should point out that they really were not of very much use.

We found that our best results were obtained when we merged the sales data with the available stock-and-debt data to get a larger sample. But we did not regard the sales data as superior to the data provided by the stock-and-debt method although it was roughly in conformity with the stock-and-debt indicator. That is the reservation, but it is a small reservation I'll grant you.

Oldman: That is very helpful to me, although it may be old stuff to everybody else here.

Capitalization Rates

Martin: I do not know. But the facts were published so that there is a possibility that most of use have become acquainted with it. Well, so much for that.

There are two ways that we approach the development of capitalization rates. I would like to comment upon the problems that each of these two methods raises. I think we ought to work on both of them for the simple reason that each of them has problems that are distinctive. And we may get better answers from one or the other in future years. I do not know. But, in defining these two methods, I am not breaking any new ground. I am simply alluding to the methods that we have, and I am undertaking to identify some of the areas for discussion within each of these two methods.

There are some particular aspects of the methodology that would seem to invite some research from people who are interested in the problem of valuation. And anyone who is interested in good valuations has to be interested in that. The first and perhaps the oldest method of doing this chore is the so-called band-of-investment approach. This term does not have a unified meaning, but it means generally that information with respect to the investment market is assembled in terms of prices of financing means that corporations typically employ so that you find the rate from the market. And, I should point out, there are some problems involved in that rather sweeping generalization. I may be overstating the case for some people that have used the band of investment, but generally speaking we find in the market a rate of capitalization that would be appropriate for common stock, preferred stock, senior bonds (classified one way or the other depending upon who is talking), and various types of junior bonds. And then, of course, you have current liabilities and deferred items that are variously handled on the liability side of your balance sheet.

Now, let me move in to the problem. The first issue that I would raise involves two aspects. The first is to reconcile definition of appraisal with actual practice. Second, and obviously this is an old statement, recognize the error of assuming the identity of the yield to an investor, which is what you measure when you take stock quotations from the market, with the cost to the utility of security capital. Now that is a different "animal," and most of the writers that I have read use this approach without differentiation. Indeed, they have usually not really addressed that problem. In a report to one of the Wichita, Kansas, conferences, the speaker made an effort to do so, but it was not an effort that seemed to be satisfactory to the man who actually did it. I think this is the best job that has been done on that, and I do not know whether you are acquainted with this document, but it is worthwhile to be acquainted with.

By the way, if you will pardon me for saying a thing that I think just has to be said in this context, it is that if we are interested in getting honest-to-goodness background studies in this matter, we need to get Ron Welch's *Carrier Taxation*. That treatise admittedly does not cover the entire waterfront, but neither does this recent study which deals only with railroad and electric utilities. Now, *Carrier Taxation* deals with more classes than that and deals with it in a much more comprehensive fashion. Ron Welch, it seems to me, made a magnificent contribution in that document, and I would recommend it to anybody who is interested in this subject. I do not know whether it is still in print, but perhaps Ron will tell us.

Welch: No, it is not in print. In fact, it has been out of print for a long, long time.

Martin: It was published in 1944, and it is a far more useful document than many of the things that we are viewing now. And it certainly could be reproduced at a reasonable cost.

What I am really driving at is this. I think that quite generally all people who have worked on the finding of the rate or a number of rates of capitalization have defined the problem of using information from the marketplace to maximum advantage; yet when it comes to the actual choices that are made, the choices seem to be influenced more by the observers' judgment about what ought to be done than what the marketplace actually says about it. Now, I think personally that this is a grave error and it needs correction.

One of these specific angles on which correction is needed is the second aspect of what I have referred to already, namely, the weighting problem that arises when one selects out and accords a given class of public service property common stock 40 percent of the total capitalization and long-term loans some other percentage and junior loans some other percentage and the miscellaneous items as still something else. It seems to me you pull the thing into a relationship that is all right for any corporation that approximates that particular capitalization structure. But you are actually using two kinds of information to do it and then are using that information in such a way that you do violence to one of them. Now if you use some kind of a concept of a typical situation to get your answer—but individual corporations to a considerable extent fail to conform in that some accord to common stock a much bigger place than 40 percent of the capital structure and others accord common stock a much smaller place in market terms—whether you fix it that way or do not, the market will change, and the market for stock does not necessarily agree with those changes, and its ups and downs do not follow the variations in the market for other types of security. Consequently, you are bound to be out of kilter if you follow a fixed percentage relationship of stock to total capitalization. And the same thing goes for senior credits—first mortgage bonds, for example.

We may say on average, such bonds constitute 23 percent of the total capital structure, but may also find that for one corporation the figure is 8 percent while for another corporation the figure is 68 percent. Now what do you do about that? My point is that the economics of the situation, which is really what we are concerned with when we ask the question, and the method of financing the property are two separate things. They are not entirely separable, you understand, because you cannot deal with one and completely exclude the other. I think that when you place as much emphasis as that on the method of financing, you are bound to distort the picture. The problem is to find some way of avoiding that result and of getting your evidence from the marketplace. If we turn that around, I could say, first, you get your evidence from the marketplace, and second, you avoid skewing the picture by the method you use in finding your rate of capitalization.

Another problem is that those students who have dealt with capitalization of earnings have for the most part undertaken to find only one rate. Ordinarily, they make a bad choice of the one rate. Ron Welch told what to do about that in 1954. At the National Tax Conference that year, there were several addresses and one of them was a paper by Ron Welch that developed what is proving, in terms of the criteria suggested a while ago, to be far and away the best in many applications. It now needs some modification to reflect some of the changes that have occurred in the balance sheets and the income statements; but still, basically speaking, the right kind of figures are used. Now, at the present time, net railway operating income or net utility operating income is showing its colors so to speak in that it is often proving itself to be technically the least satisfactory measure of income for capitalization purposes. Many students have pointed out that net operating income has a weakness mainly because it mixes the expenses of nonoperating property with expenses of operating property for most classes of the public service corporations, notably railroads. I think this occurs for all classes, but there are some that ostensibly make a separation, for example, airlines and natural gas pipelines.

The other scheme for an attack on this problem is the scheme of multiple methods of capitalization chosen from a much larger number of attempts. For example, in a project that is nearing completion, we have reviewed eleven different capitalization levels for railroads. We have come up with four that seem to yield reasonable results. The least accurate in the case of railroads, as expected, is the net railway operating income. I should state here that we would not even use net railway operating income at all if it were not for the fact that we have been able to provide a modification that improves it by eliminating one of the sources of error introduced by the recent changes in income statements. As a matter of fact, we made the same change in all of the rates. So whatever rate we have among those four one of which is almost identical with the Welch suggestion of twenty years ago except for that modification; that one is the best. It would have three times the weighting of the net railway operating income capitalization rate. So it would actually be about one-third of the total of the four rates.

Reeves: Well said, Dr. Martin. Now let us turn to the junior member of our distinguished triumvirate, Ron Welch.

Determining Capitalization Rates

Welch: The previous speakers have thrown out some very stimulating thoughts, and a number of items they have suggested are worthy of our exploration. For the moment, I would like to address myself to methods of determining rates of capitalization and leave the many problems involved in the valuation of railroads and other public utility properties for subsequent discussion. All who are interested in the complex field of appraisal are well aware of the three methods of developing a rate of capitalization. There is the summation approach that starts with a safe interest rate and adds elements for risk, nonliquidity and other factors. Most people reject this particular approach in that it is very difficult to support. The safe rate can be determined with some degree of satisfaction, but the rest of the elements are largely fictitious. So I do not think anybody gives much credence to that particular method of deriving a rate of capitalization.

The market-determined rate, on the other hand, is a rate derived by the preferred method but is hardly useful in the particular field in which we are involved—that of railroad and utility valuation. There generally are not enough sales to relate earnings to selling price to determine a direct or market rate of capitalization. The market-derived rate of capitalization has another problem that I think is sometimes overlooked. We really have to ask ourselves what the buyer of the property anticipated in the way of earnings. We do not know this, so we assume that the prior earnings should be capitalized, and this really is not so at all. I ran into this problem head-on in connection with a valuation of some cable television systems, where there was a great deal of cable television plant installed, but the actual records of the company indicated the systems were losing money. If you try to develop a direct or market rate of capitalization for properties that are losing money, you cannot do it by relating past earnings to sales prices. Obviously, the people who are buying properties of that kind are not buying prior earnings; they are buying future earnings, as everyone who is a student of valuation would know. These buyers are saying to themselves that the future will be much more profitable than the past.

When you get right down to it, the band-of-investment approach is the only method left for constructing capitalization rates for the kinds of property that we are talking about here. But even this method has a number of problems associated with it. In its simplest terms, all that one does is to decide what particular portion of capital falls into each of the various categories that Jim Martin referred to earlier—as many as a half dozen different categories if you choose all possibilities. Most people do not develop quite that much detail and use only three or four. You may have bonds, preferred stock, and common stock, but you probably do not need to go into much greater detail than that, although I recall in the NATA report of the Committee on Unit Valuation, which I had a small hand in, we did add equipment trust certificates, and we even put in something else that is an interesting innovation—at least I have not seen it in any other literature—and that was current liabilities. And I might say a word or two about this item before I conclude my remarks.

There are two particular problems associated with the band-of-investment method of developing capitalization rates. One is the proportions that you are going to use, and the other is the rate that you associate with each portion. When you have answered those two questions, the rest of the derivation flows with mathematical certainty. If, for example, you have decided that the bonds ought to be 60 percent, the preferred stock 10 percent, and the common stock 30 percent (and ignore current liabilities because most people do not recognize them as another category) and then you have associated certain yield rates with these various categories, you simply take a weighted average of the yield rates using capital structure percentages for weighting. It is not too difficult, in my judgment, to develop a rate for the bonds, or for the preferred stock for that matter. Most of the problem with this method, as I see it, comes in connection with the common stock rate.

But before even discussing the rate of return for common stock, I should ask how to develop the percentages for proportioning the capital structure. There are two basic methods that are used, I believe. One is to look at the balance sheets of other companies within the same industry—making sure that they are reasonably comparable with the property that you are valuing—and average the percentages of book value for each type of capital. There is, however, an alternative approach in which you do not use the book values at all, but you use the market values. This is a more difficult approach because it is quite likely many of the companies that are being used for this purpose are not located in the area in which you are appraising, and it becomes quite a burden to apply the market value approach. You have to make virtually a stock-and-debt appraisal of the companies that you are not trying to appraise at all but are only trying to use for comparison to develop a capitalization rate. If the common stock is valued on the books at $25 a share, but the market says that it is only worth $10 a share, you use the $10 figure to determine what the common stock proportion should be. I thought that was the right answer until a short time ago, when it dawned on me that we may not be interested in either one of these two things.

The reason I found that to be the case was that I was apprasing a cable television company and several of the cable television companies for which financial data are available have reported net operating losses over the years, with the result that the book value of their common stock has been reduced very substantially by these cumulative deficits. So, what relevance does the book value have? For that matter, what relevance does the market value, which might reflect these deficits even more clearly, have? What you are really asking yourself is how a purchaser would finance the pruchase. How would a person coming in to acquire ownership of the property being appraised divide his capital investment among the various kinds of debt and equity securities? I do not think either the book value or the market value of the existing capital structure gives you an answer to this question. Unfortunately, that leaves me with virtually no answer at all, which is a very unsatisfactory but a fairly common experience in the field of utility valuation.

The only thing that I can think of that you might do in this connection would be to interview investment bankers and brokers who handle this type of property if there are such. There happen to be some in the cable television field because there are more than 3,000 cable television systems operating now, and some of these are being bought and sold from time to time. So there is the possibility of getting an informed opinion from people who are in that market as to how you might finance a purchase of a cable television system. I spoke with one person who has been doing some buying and selling in the field of cable television, and I asked him what kind of financing would be likely to occur. He gave me an answer that may be worth something or may be worth nothing. I think it may be superior to some of the things that we have been doing, and I think his answer was a reasonable one. Anyhow, he suggests that you must make some kind of a division of the capital that you think would be consistent with the proportions employed by a likely purchaser of the property.

Next, you must ascribe some rates of return to the various elements of the capital structure. You do not have a really big problem with bonds it seems to me. If you are dealing with a railroad, you can get rates of return on various classes of railroad bonds and come up with a reasonably good judgment as to what rate of return one should attach to them. Preferred stock yields are about as easily analyzed. But what do you do about the common stock? I agree, I believe, with Jim Martin's approach on this part of the capital structure. However, I am not sure that I am clear on exactly what he was saying about the rate of return on common stocks, so I will be interested in his reaction to my remarks. It seems to me that you have to see what the market indicates as the proper return for common stock. The book value, in my judgment, is meaningless in this area, although I am not sure that Don Fisher will agree with me, and I am quite certain that Judd Eastman does not. I think that what you have to do is look to the earnings-price ratio for companies that are of a similar nature to the one that you are appraising and say to yourself that a person who is financing a purchase of this kind of an enterprise would appear to be able, based upon the prices now being paid for stock, to sell stock that would yield the investor the same earnings-price ratio obtained by a similar group of stocks in the stock market. This procedure, of course, assumes that the earnings that you are using for this earnings-price ratio are at a rate that is reasonably representative of the future, for, as you well know, a person buying stock is buying the future, not the past. So this concept is useful, I would think, only for companies with fairly stable incomes. You have to assume that the future is going to be pretty much like the recent past. That assumption is not too bad for some of the utility properties. But it may not be very good for some of the railroads, and it certainly is not very good for cable television.

You have probably heard of the beta factor, which is an empirical method that investment counselors use in trying to decide what sort of price one would be justified in paying for a stock. These counselors take an earnings-price ratio for one company or one line of business, and they modify this to reflect differences in risks that are associated with the more risky types of enterprises, but essentially they are using the market price as their touchstone.

I referred to an innovation that appeared in the NATA Committee report—ascribing a rate of return to current liabilities. Of course, the current liabilities do not have any explicit rates of return, but, in our NATA report, we arbitrarily used 2 percent. With the kind of rates in today's market, 2 percent may no longer be appropriate; perhaps it should be 5 percent now. The theory is that you do not have to pay for things the minute you buy them, but you do incur the current liability because you have unpaid bills. You do not pay your wages daily or hourly; you pay your wages at the end of a two-week period or perhaps a month's period of time or whatever happens to be your policy. You do not pay for your supplies immediately; you pay for them thirty days after billing. And some place in what you pay for those things, there has to be a hidden interest charge. So the NATA Committee included 2 percent of the face value of current liabilities to be capitalized and put a current liabilities yield rate into the capitalization rate.

You can rationalize that point, the NATA Committee's innovation not only in the manner that I have just suggested a few moments ago, but also by looking at what you do with the stock-and-debt approach. In the stock-and-debt approach, despite what I consider unreasonable dissent, we do use current liabilities. We put current liabilities into our stock-and-debt indicators of value, and if you are going to make the stock-and-debt approach parallel to the income approach, as I think you should, then you are going to have to put some amount in what Jim Martin calls the capitalization rate base and in the capitalization rate as a return on current liabilities. Lacking that, if everything else were to work perfectly, the stock-and-debt value would always come out in excess of the capitalized income value and logic tells me that if you do everything perfect in employing two different approaches to value, you ought to come out with the same answer and not with two answers that could not possibly be the same. For that reason, I think there is a lot of virtue in including current liabilities in the capital structure, although I admit you may have to be quite arbitrary in ascribing the proper interest rate for this element and the degree of arbitrariness may contribute to the contention that the method lacks virtue.

These are the remarks that I would like to contribute to the discussion on the band-of-investment method of developing a capitalization rate, and if someone can tell me how to come up with answers to some of my questions, I would be very happy to hear them.

McSwain: Mr. Welch, I would like to ask a few questions about your presentation. If we take your example of the way in which we derive a rate of capitalization by the band-of-investment method and assume the price earnings ratio is 12, then the reciprocal would be 8.5. And, in your comment, you have 8.5 instead of 12. And that certainly is not an uncommon figure. Now if you have your bonds showing a return of 10 percent and your preferred stock showing a return of 11 percent, my question is: Can you justify a return to common equity of 8.5 percent?

Welch: I agree that is a very common situation. We just seem to take it for granted that common stock must have a higher rate of return than debt. I think it reflects the fact that the investing public does not regard the past income as indicative of the probable future income. And, therefore, even though they are discounting their prospective future income at a higher rate than the bond rate or preferred stock rate, the ratio of past earnings to current stock price may be lower than the yield rate on bonds.

McSwain: Is it possible that this could be the problem? What we are supposedly doing is appraising the property for ad valorem tax purposes as of a given date and I cannot say that I know for sure that this holds true now, but a couple of years ago we made a study of dividend payout per share and the results indicated that these two items were up rather substantially. It may be that a common stock purchaser is not only looking for profit on his immediate investment, but the leverage brought about by additional property that will be earning in the future. Actually, he is looking at appreciation of his investment pretty much in the same way that someone who buys a farm now with our current high interest rates will actually purchase a property that will yield a net current return of 3 percent a year. In actuality, he is looking at the future anticipated increments in the value of that property. If we find an 8 percent return on equity, by using a price-earnings ratio, should we be making an adjustment to take out the future anticipated increments of the property value since we are actually appraising the property as of this particular date?

Welch: I think you have raised two questions there, Bob. One is whether you are appraising property that is not yet in existence. I think that is an entirely different question than the one in your illustration of the farm, where you are appraising property that *is* already in existence and is producing an income stream that is expected to grow rather than remain constant. I have heard the first question—the one involving additional property—frequently. Joel Stern made quite a point of it in his talks at our Western States Association of Tax Administrators conference on capital markets a couple of years ago. The stock-and-debt value may include stock prices that are high because the market anticipates new investments in property, which is going to produce more income per dollar of investment than the existing property is producing. To the extent that that situation does exist, the stock-and-debt indicator of value will include the value of property not presently in existence. I am not satisfied that this occurs with enough frequency or in enough volume among public utility companies to become a problem that should be of great concern to appraisers.

McSwain: Once I had an occasion to appraise a Florida telephone company located in the Orlando area. At that time, telephone stocks were selling for somewhere between twelve and fifteen times earnings. Yet the stock of that particular company was selling for twenty-five times earnings. And, of course, the investors who were paying twenty-five times earnings for that stock were looking for future growth of that particular telephone company. So I think in that particular situation, there is no question about what anticipation of future growth entered into the purchasing decisions of the shareholders.

Welch: I would not deny that there might be instances of this type. However, I think it is a rather unusual instance because of the very stringent regulations under which these particular companies must operate.

McSwain: But in my illustration the investors had accepted an 8.5 percent return on common stock, which was less than the return on bonds and preferred stock. And, in that case, you said they were looking at anticipated future income. They were actually looking at the future income stream. But under a strictly regulated public utility commission, the only way they can get increased revenues is through the expansion of their physical facilities. So would that not in itself tell you that this anticipation that they are looking forward to is going to come about through an expansion of the plant at some future date?

Welch: It is my impression, Bob—and you probably know much better than I do because you have been a practicing appraiser in this field for many, many years— that in the last few years earnings-price ratios were slightly in excess of the yield rates on bonds rather than substantially lower. Am I right about that?

McSwain: It depends on the type of utility. In some of them the returns are substantially less for common stock than for bonds. When the current cost of money was at about 10 percent, we found many in which the reciprocal of the price-earnings ratio was around seven or eight. And it is hard for me to justify a 7.5 percent or 8 percent return on the equity of a regulated company position when the funded debt was around 10 percent and the preferred stock was re-turning about the same. In fact, in one company the bonds went to 13 percent, and when we looked at the reciprocal of the price-earnings ratio for common stock, that reciprocal was down around eight indicating an 8 percent return. So actually the bond rates were about five points greater than the rate of return to common equity.

Welch: That may be true, but that was for one company. What about the figures for the industry itself? When you are working up a band-of-investment capitali-zation rate, you do not concern yourself only with the company you are apprais-ing. You must be concerned with the industry as a whole—or at least with substantial segments of the industry.

Reeves: I wish somebody would explain to me why we should do this.

McSwain: Me too. But I still have some more questions I would like to ask. One of them is about your band-of-investment approach used to develop a rate of capitalization. There is an item on the liability side of the balance sheet that is usually equal to or greater than current liabilities. And that item is deferred credits. This is caused by the deferral of federal income tax. Many regulatory commissions for rate-making purposes show this item as part of the capital structure. They show no interest or no cost attached to the deferred income tax. This actually reduces the capitalization rate because in effect it is an interest-free loan. That is how I view the matter. Do you think it is reasonable to throw deferred income tax in as another component but show no interest for the item and thereby bring about a reduced rate of capitalization?

Welch: I must admit that I have experienced a certain amount of confusion about what to do with that particular item. At the California Board of Equaliza-tion, we wrote a rule on the stock-and-debt approach to value but did not adopt it because the assessors in California were so opposed to it—and they asked "Who needs it?" The answer was we needed it, and we thought they needed it too, sometimes but not often. With a politically oriented board, our values did not seem to have much appeal. Anyway, I think that I would like to run our draft of this proposed rule past some practitioners in the field to see whether it conforms to their thinking, particularly about the method of handling deferred items.

McSwain: At one time, it was not a major problem, but since the federal government now allows accelerated depreciation, investment tax credits, and other items, these items have substantial effects on the balance sheet.

Welch: That is true. Here is what we said in the California Board of Equalization about current liabilities for whatever light it can throw upon your question: "The current liabilities to be valued are those current and deferred liabilities that are actual legal obligations (other than declared but unpaid dividends that contribute to the market value of the stock). The market values of these debts is indicated by their face or book value in the absence of evidence to the contrary. Contingent liabilities should be excluded unless there is evidence that they represent actual legal obligations." Admittedly, this may be something that we do simply because we do not know what else to do. The really important part of the statement is this: "The objective is to include any obligation that purchasers of the total equity interest would assume at the actual amount the purchaser would reduce the price he pays for the equity interest by reason of the obligations assumed." It is like buying a home with a mortgage on it. How much less did you pay for the property by reason of the fact that the mortgage was already in existence? I guess I really do not know the answer to your question, Bob.

Deferred Federal Income Tax

McSwain: Well, the Accounting Board disagrees with me, and they so state in their accounting regulations. But I have a feeling that this deferred federal income tax is to a very large extent a surplus item that is set aside in a special category for financial reporting purposes. This is something that someone might have to pay back sometime in the future. But, at one time, they just flowed it through. In fact, the Interstate Commerce Commission just changed its rules of reporting two years ago, and it is my impression that when this item was allowed as a flow-through item, it could have been used for any purpose. But then some of the financial people said: "Look here, we might be making a mistake by allowing you to paint the financial picture with too rosy a glow." Because by flowing this through, it becomes reflected in your reported earnings per share, but in actuality you might have to pay this tax at some time in the future. So let us just be careful about how rosy a glow we put on our current financial reporting. It might be well just to set this aside and let the people who read your financial statements be aware of the fact that this is something that they might have to pay back at some uncertain future date. So even though the Accounting Board says it is not surplus and that it is a true deferred credit, I must say I sometimes have my doubts as to whether it is a true liability that is more or less just a setting aside of part of the surplus.

Welch: Well, let us hear from Don Fisher, who has faced this particular problem and seems to have solved it at least to his own satisfaction.

Fisher: I think that if you went to the Internal Revenue Service they would tell you that they never conceived of this as anything other than a debt that was due and owed Uncle Sam and that some day you are going to have to pay it back.

McSwain: Well, I just lost a case down in Mobile, and the judge there said it was not a liability in any way.

Fisher: Well, in that case I would have to respectfully disagree with your judicial branch of government. But we have some of those decisions in our part of the country too. I am sometimes at a loss to explain how they are reached. We may have to come back and face the horrible reality that either our attorneys or appraisers simply did an inadequate job of demonstrating matters to the members of the judicial system. But we treat this, I think, as a true debt. It is an element that has a zero interest rate component in your band-of-investment calculation of a capitalization rate. However, we would add it in as part of the stock-and-debt value. We would discount it today and say that its present value is not the book value, but it would be based upon future payments. We in Oregon have coped with that as far back as 1950, when they had defense plant certificates and they were allowed to accelerate the amortization of Copco's Big Plant and some of the other Pacific Power and Light hydroplants. This meant they could write off nearly 65 percent of that investment in a five-year period. This gave us big accelerated depreciation very early in the life of the plant and very little depreciation over the later years of the plant's life. We set this item up right away as a deferral item with a payback feature, and we even allow them to give us a schedule on how they are going to pay this back in future years. We just discounted that to its present worth and took that as the value of that item on the liability side. It was actually the present worth of that liability as if you were going to have to satisfy it. We are treating deferred federal income tax in the same way right now. In fact, we made a presentation for the Western States Tax Administrators' meeting, and I also have the unfortunate opportunity of presenting it in Wichita at the Railroad and Utility Valuation Workshop again this year. It is ironical that Pacific Power and Light has us in court on a matter of treating deferred federal income tax as an additional stream of income, which is exactly what we did. We say to them that since you did not pay this much as a tax item, we are going to add it to the potential income stream that a prospective purchaser would visualize receiving. And the company has said generally, "You are fooling around with the income statement and you just cannot do that." This year we did something a little bit different. We said, "Okay, we will treat that deferred federal income tax as if it were contributed capital, and we will leave it outside of the unit, and we will find our values without any consideration of deferred federal income tax. We will find the unit value and then we will add in this property that you have bought with this contributed capital." Other companies have said, "We understand that. It is perfectly all right." It actually produces the same results, but one place we are tinkering with the income statement and another place we are calling it contributed capital as though it were contributions in aid of construction. So they seem to understand that approach but they do not understand the earlier approach of adjusting the income statement.[b]

Debt-Equity Ratios

Reeves: Arlo Woolery, do you have a question?

Woolery: I would like to ask Ron a theoretical question involving the band-of-investment method of deriving a rate of capitalization. If you were to go to a capital structure that had 95 percent debt and only 5 percent equity, pretty obviously your company would be worth a great deal more than one with 60 percent debt and 40 percent equity because you would have a lower rate of capitalization. So, are we to infer from this that the more debt your company has, the more valuable it becomes?

Welch: If theory just worked out perfectly, it would seem that these two things—the percentage of debt in the capital structure and the yield rate on the debt—ought to compensate for each other. If you want to capitalize with 90 percent debt, you would very likely pay a higher rate of interest on that debt than if you had only 60 percent debt in your capital structure because you would have a great deal more security with a lower debt percentage. But I do not suppose anything ever works out that perfectly.

I have to come back to my position that you are not concerned about the capital structure of the company you are appraising and that your real concern is with the purchaser and how he would finance his purchase. How would the most likely purchaser proceed in setting up the capital structure to finance his

---

[b]See Appendix B.

acquisition? And I must point out that this is a hypothetical purchaser, a purely hypothetical one. He is not someone who could finance the acquisition by reason of his own personal credit. But he is going to finance the purchase in a manner that is typical for this particular type of enterprise, and if it happens to be an enterprise that could typically be financed 90 percent by borrowing and 10 percent by equity investment, I would have to say that this is a more valuable property than one that is typically financed by 60 percent debt and 40 percent equity. The latter has a higher degree of risk associated with it and therefore is less valuable.

Incidentally, this is not a new question to those of us who have been working with railroad valuations in California. We have had some of these same questions raised on the value indicated by capitalization of income. As a matter of fact, the same question has surfaced with the Santa Fe railroad valuation for many years. The railroad says that the use of the theoretical distribution of capital between funded debt and equity is not right—that we should actually use the company's own distribution of these capital elements. The Santa Fe has a considerably higher equity content in its capital structure than is typical for the railroad industry. So when using the industry's typical capital structure, we wind up ascribing to the Santa Fe a somewhat larger debt component than actually exists in the company's capital structure, and the railroad feels that it is unjust to do so. We said, "No, that is not really the question. We are not concerned about the capital structure in your own company. We are concerned with what the capital structure of a prospective purchaser would be when buying your company." So, we say that the Santa Fe is actually worth more than the company thinks because in our capitalization rate derivation, we give them a lower equity percentage in the band of investment.

Reeves: What about the seller, Ron?

Welch: Well, I am really not concerned about the seller. I am only concerned about the purchaser.

Martin: But that's not economics. Both parties are important to an transaction.

Welch: The seller is important only in the sense that the use value that Mr. Bonbright spoke about earlier comes into play. I think the question really is, what could you sell the property for? If you are actually a willing seller, what will you receive for your property when you sell it? Now some people may not be willing to sell. They are not the marginal owners. But I say, let's not pay any attention to the seller. And the reason I say that is because what I think we are looking for is what happens in the marketplace between people who sell and people who buy. It is true that every seller has a withholding price, and he is not willing to sell below that particular price level. The transaction actually occurs when the offering price of some buyer meets his withholding price, and at that point, I think that the buyer and seller become almost interchangeable. So by looking into the characteristics of the purchaser, you have identified the essential characteristics of the seller.

Martin: I thought that was what you were driving at in the first place. I do not think I have any big argument with you. However, if you are speaking of the purchaser with no reference at all to the seller, then I would have to feel that you are doing so at your own peril. It seems to me the seller has to participate in the transaction.

Welch: Yes, he has to be willing to sell, but I do not think that the capital structure of the seller is important because his capital is sunk. It is the capital of the purchaser that is not sunk. So, in my opinion, the capital structure of the existing company is immaterial. I may seem to be saying these things in a very positive manner, but I am not really as certain of myself as I may sound.

Oldman: Is it useful in thinking about this problem to note that from the point of view of the seller you are actually talking about cash equivalents? To him what you are really talking about is reducing all of these financing means used by the purchaser to cash equivalents coming to the seller and that is the price that you are finally talking about. And that is why focusing, as Ron does, on how the purchaser would finance getting the cash for the seller is really the relevant thing. That is why I do not think you have to talk about the seller at all. I think that is just another way of saying what Ron has been saying right along.

Reeves: Clarence Brasfield has a comment at this point.

Brasfield: Yes, a comment that is mostly a question. It is in connection with the question of the employment of a higher debt ratio than the one actually in existence for a company. It seems to me that if this came about, you would be compelled to go back and look at the cost of debt. For instance, if a company is AAA rated with its existing debt-equity ratio and then has sufficient interest coverage to maintain that, you would have a change in circumstances if you were to ascribe a higher debt ratio to that company because then you would have to recognize the fact that its debt would become more costly. You would have to ascribe a higher debt cost at the same time—that is, I mean a higher debt cost than that actually in existence with the ratio as it stands at the present time.

Welch: You are absolutely right about that, and I do not know how pure we have been in recognizing your point in the past.

McSwain: I disagree with Ron and his theory that we should use a capital structure that is typical for a given industry. I think that when we deal with normal appraisal practice, we are dealing with properties that can be easily refinanced. If we go out and buy an apartment building that may cost $1.5 million, we can always finance that $1.5 million, and we can develop a capital structure that meets the needs of a financer and would be typical in the marketplace. But when you are deailing with a property like a railroad or something similar that may have $1.5 billion worth of stock and long-term debts outstanding, I just do not think there are many opportunities to refinance.

I also think there is another problem that you have when you are talking about rearranging a public utilities capital structure. Railroads, of course, are not regulated to a strict rate base concept, but when we are talking about public utilities in general, I think the public service commissions or the regulatory commissions would not approve the rearranging of a capital structure to that typical of the industry unless that rearrangement provided a certain advantage to the consumer. If the resulting financial structure did make the company in question typical of the industry, but brought about higher consumer costs, I do not think the regulatory commission would approve of that transaction simply because of the impact on the customers of the utility.

But I think the main question is the difference between taking a $1 million or $1.5 million financial deal and setting up any structure you want and the greatly increased problems of talking about a $1.5 billion financial transaction where there is no feasible way to rearrange the financial structure along the lines that are thought to be typical for the industry. So, I like to look at each individual company I am appraising, and then I compute the capital structure of that individual company and then go through the steps for developing a band-of-investment rate of capitalization.

Welch: Bob, it may become theoretical when you are talking about restructuring the capital ratios of a huge corporation. I suppose you can argue that it would be inequitable to assume a restructuring when this type of restructuring is not in the cards. On the other hand, there are lots of aspects of property taxation that are somewhat theoretical. For example, when you have a property that is subject to a lease, you do not take account of the lease in the valuation concept. You ask yourself what the property would sell for if it did not have the lease on it, and you may say that the lease actually creates a hardship if the price is higher than it would have been without the lease. There is also the possibility of an adverse lease in which you stick the owner with a higher valuation simply because the property is leased at what has turned out to be an uneconomic rental figure. We do have a number of situations in the property tax field where we may breach some of our common concepts of equity, and I do not know whether they are justified.

As I said before, I do not intend to be dogmatic about these things because I think dogmatism is about the last thing that we need to inject into the world of valuation. But this is the way we have done it, and we thought we were justified in doing it this way. If other people feel differently about the matter, I am certainly not about to say that they are wrong and that we are right.

Capital Structure

Reeves: I think that Tom Fleming has a question.

Fleming: Actually, Bob McSwain asked about three-fourths of my question concerning the restructuring of the capitalization ratios when calculating the band-of-investment capitalization rate. I would like to follow along and pursue the income side of the question. Do we also have to consider restructuring the income stream to be typical of the industry for which the company is a part? Do you set up a typical model and apply this typical structure to the company that we are valuing in spite of the fact that it derives its income through the regulatory process that is not based on the typical model but is based upon the company's existing structure? I think my question also covers Clarence Brasfield's question about the company's cost of debt based upon its capital structure and its income stream—that is, one type of company that is strictly regulated as to rate base and rate of return, and then you have railroads that do not have established rate bases but are regulated on an entirely different basis. I have a great deal more trouble in applying the typical capital structure concept to the strictly regulated companies or to the rate base determination than I do in applying the concept of a typical capital structure to a company that is not regulated on a typical rate base concept.

However, that brings up another problem involving companies that are not regulated on a rate base concept. It is this big $1.5 billion corporation that Bob McSwain was talking about in which it does not seem practical or feasible to change the capital structure. I have trouble putting it all together and comparing it to this typical model and relating everything to the company that I have to value. I just throw that out as a question and a comment to illustrate a practical problem that I happen to run into and would appreciate any comments.

Welch: In my preliminary remarks I said that if the stock-and-debt approach works perfectly and the income approach works perfectly, you ought to come up with the same answers for the same property. In a sense I am then renouncing the typical purchaser concept because the stock-and-debt approach does deal with the particular capital structure of the company being appraised; if this capital structure is very different from that of a prospective purchaser, you will have to come up with different answers. However, this is not all bad. There may be some virtue in having two approaches that will produce two different answers. I remember that Harley Lutz once in one of his writings condemned the stock-and-debt approach on the grounds that it was just a duplicate of the capitalized income approach. He said that in effect you are just giving double weight to the capitalization of income as an indicator of value. I do not remember whether he was trying to condemn the indefensible method of assessment that was being used by the state of New Jersey at that time but, if memory serves me right, that is exactly what he said. In any event, if you use the method of capitalization of income that I expounded, you will come out with a different answer than you will with the stock-and-debt approach unless the capital structure of the company you are appraising is typical.

McDougall: I would like to take a step backward to an earlier question that revolved about the idea that the appraiser would like to have the estimate of value be independent of the financial structure of the company. I have the impression that there may be some confusion over the matter of finding "the value" of a company as compared with a reported value of a company. I would suggest that perhaps there is really no such thing as "the value" (intrinsic value). I would also like to go back to Bob's point. In some instances, I do not think you can determine a value independent of the financial structure since they are intimately tied together; you can never divorce yourself from that financial structure. Thus, when a person purchases an income stream, he also purchases the financial structure that provided the wherewithal to produce that income stream. It may be a convenient theoretical abstraction to think that you can change the financial structure when in fact it is somewhat fixed. This suggests that you should perhaps take this into account in the valuation process.

I have one other comment on your inclusion of current liabilities. Perhaps you could be a little more positive by making a statement such as this: My current liabilities include a premium payment that is equal to the real short-term interest rate. And this would be true whether it be a thirty-day account or a sixty- or ninety-day note. Then use this actual rate instead of saying it is arbitrary.

Welch: You may very well be right. I really have not thought about this particular problem for quite a long time. As a matter of fact, we never did follow that part of the NATA Committee's recommendations in California.

Reeves: I think we are anxious to get others' reactions at this point—specifically on this problem of whether you use the capital structure of the present operating company or the capital structure that would be typical of the industry that company represents. Would you like to comment on that, Professor Bonbright?

Bonbright: Well, I have not thought a great deal about that particular question, but I find the whole matter very interesting. When I think in terms of taking the existing capitalization and restructuring it to fit the capital structure of a willing buyer, I am persuaded that we are getting right to market value. And this gets us away from the concept of valuing the company on the basis of what it is worth to the present owner. I should ask as a follow-up: Are you making any assumptions as to the incidence of the tax in the case of a regulated utility, which in many cases fairly promptly passes on, within limits, any increase in tax to the consumers, or are you disregarding that? I guess I am asking are you not paying any attention to that, or are you making at least the assumption that the buyers of electricity will be the people eventually paying the property tax?

Welch: No, we are not making any assumptions regarding the incidence of the property tax. I will be willing to take a position on that, but we did not really consider it to be a relevant issue.

Oldman: It seems to me there is an easy way of clarifying this point. If you will remember, a while back Ron brought up the analogy of a long-term adverse or favorable lease. I do not think that particular item was pursued enough, and one way of restating this would be to say that for property tax purposes the objective from an equity point of view may be that two different utility companies ought to pay the same amount of property tax. They have basically the same physical equipment just as you would say with respect to two buildings that are physically the same, but have different leases—one a favorable long-term lease and one an adverse long-term lease. For property tax purposes, equity demands, at least in the minds of some of us, that the property tax be the same on those two properties and the investors through their contractual arrangements with financiers or lessees take the risks involved with their contracts. But the property taxpayers should not be affected by that at all. If you regard that as your philosophy of the property tax, then it seems to me you cannot escape from Ron's approach, and you will have to admit that Ron's approach is the only correct one theoretically. The only objections could be the practical ones that have been raised, which seem to me are real objections and raise a lot of questions about how you convert Ron's method into an operating reality. I do not know whether this helps clarify anything, but it does seem to me that this is what we are really talking about here.

McSwain: Maybe, but that raises another question. Even though you do that and wind up with the capital structure part equalized, you still must look at the company's actual rates, which are based on its actual capital structure. When you do this, you change the rate of return for various elements and throw it out of kilter again.

Fisher: You are going too far behind the scene, Bob. You have to stop at that first theoretical thing. What would a prospective purchaser today do in financing his purchase? I think one of the things we are losing sight of is the approach. When we get over here on cloud nine, we get too far away from it. The cost approach is basically an approach through the principle of substitution. What would we substitute for these properties? The income approach is theoretically what an investor would pay for these things. The stock-and-debt approach is still another indication of what he would pay. What would be the value in exchange if you could assume that the market prices of the total outstanding stock and debt is equivalent to a sales transaction? But each one of these approaches is running into valuation problems in three distinctive ways. In a certain sense they are not compatible. We know where we are headed. Our target is market value. So all these approaches are pseudo approaches to that because we have nothing else to go with.

McSwain: Oh, I was going to ask Ron what he meant when he made a statement earlier that we could not get a meaningful value for the whole property. At one time I thought I was a pretty good railroad appraiser, but the longer I work at it, I find that I know less and less about it. I know that I cannot raise my hand and swear that I have determined a value of the fifteen railroads operating in Alabama. So do you feel, Ron, that you have a meaningful value when you do a railroad appraisal?

Welch: I said I do not think we have a *meaningless* value.

Bonbright: But what do you do with a railroad that has a lot of value that lies outside of the operating unit—let's say a company with nonoperating property like timber or maybe oil wells, such as Union Pacific?

Welch: I agree with Jim Martin that we are being reduced more and more to the single approach of capitalized income. You can allocate income with some degree of certainty among the various operations. Sure, you cannot make a perfect allocation but you can generally allocate the gross revenue fairly accurately, and then the question of how you allocate the expenses becomes a more or less answerable question. So if you can segregate the income, the income approach produces the answer that you are looking for. The very activities that you speak of certainly detract from the usefulness of the stock-and-debt approach. And then if you are operating in an area where the cost approach is useless, which I think is generally true of railroads—not always, but generally speaking—you have just the income approach left. It is the only thing you can work with, imperfect as it may be.

McSwain: I would like to come back to another statement made a few minutes ago in which we took the capital structure and ran it up to 95 percent funded debt and 5 percent common equity and then asked whether you have a more valuable railroad. But I would like to point out that value is based upon risk, and if you change the capital structure, you change the risk element. And you could wind up with exactly the same capitalization rate in either case, and there would not be any advantage in rearranging the capital structure.

Welch: I agree with you, but let me restate my position. I said that if the typical capital structure of any particular line of enterprise was 90 percent debt and 10 percent equity and a typical capital structure for some other line of enterprise was 60 percent debt and 40 percent equity, then the first property has a greater value than the second because it is risk free. If you are able to borrow 90 percent of the capital value, then it must be a relatively risk-free enterprise, and so it has to be a more valuable property per dollar of income than the one with a typical 60 percent debt and 40 percent equity capital structure.

Bonbright: How about valuing properties that are already in receivership?

Welch: We have enough problems without getting into that, but I would be happy to defer to anyone who has ever valued such a property.

Reeves: The way things are going in the railroad industry, people are going to have to get some experience in doing just that. Arlo, do you think that your question has been responded to adequately or do you want to get in one last word on this particular subject?

Woolery: I think I see my question in better perspective now. Thanks to Clarence, Bob, Ron, and Professor Bonbright. It seems to me our answer boils down to this: That if you did go to a capital structure that was 90 percent debt and 10 percent equity, the very thin equity would be in an extremely high-risk position as far as the equity owner is concerned because a small shift in the company situation could wipe out the 10 percent equity. So I feel that what Ron is saying is that if you take bonds at 10 percent interest with a 90 percent capitalization ratio, the remaining 10 percent equity is going to be looking for a 60 percent or 70 percent annual return because of the exposure, and when you start calculating your band-of-investment cap rate on this particular basis, you will wind up with the same rate of capitalization.

McSwain: Of course, your bond rates would have to be higher than normal, too, with that large a percentage of your capitalization in bonded indebtedness. So that would tend to offset the higher percentage of the capitalization in funded debt. I think that Clarence Brasfield's thoughts about the change in bond rating and interest coverage gets into that particular area and covers that argument very well.

Martin: It seems to me that in a fairly considerable number of cases, that depends upon the functional characteristics of a particular utility and they vary within themselves. I think my point of view duplicates what has been said, and I think the conclusion that the rate of capitalization for any given company or any given industry reflects the investor attitude toward the risk involved in investing in that particular company or industry. And those investor attitudes to a certain extent may be independent of the actual capital structure of the industry or company.

There are some other problems that may attach to this particular discussion. One is that there are some railroads, for example, that have functions that are different from the typical functions of what we call "railroads." The one that occurs to me right now is the Richmond-Fredericksburg and Potomac, which has the job of getting a good deal of freight delivered in Richmond in place of what used to be the Seaboard, the Coastline, and the Southern into Washington and some of it into New York over the old Pennsylvania line. Now the capitalization structure of the RF&P, because of that peculiar function and the regularity of its business as compared with the roads that are bringing the freight to it, makes it possible for the company to have a capital structure that is far different from the typical railroad. It is very heavily indebted; yet every year it comes through with quite reasonable earnings on the equity. Now this is just one side of the thing.

I would like to make another point that may already have been made by Ron Welch better than I can make it. But it seems to me that an illustration will help shed some light on the matter. If you assume when buying a duplex that is already well financed that you get a first mortgage bond for a very sizable portion of the total, that is better, all other things being equal, than if a buyer does not get that type of financing and has to find cash in the open market to finance the whole thing. If you do that in the case of a simple duplex, how do you avoid doing it in the case of a complex railroad system, a complex electric power system, or what have you in the utility field?

Another point was touched upon but not fully discussed a while ago, and that is the differences in regulatory schemes that are very real and very fundamental to the income-producing capacity of the taxpayer.

These are questions that do arise and you may think, and probably will say, that you do not know the answers, but it seems to me that we ought to face these questions. A lot of things are question marks, and that should be our clue to start looking for answers to them.

Brasfield: In our company we think in terms of two types of risks—financial risk and business risk. For instance, we would say that the highly leveraged company represents a high financial risk. If we compare our company to the electric utilities, generally they are higher leveraged companies than the telephone companies. So we would say that the financial risk would be greater for the electric companies. Now from the category of business risk, we say that telephone companies have a higher risk because of the fact that downturns in the economy take the real cream of our revenues and affect our revenues in the most profitable areas, if there is such a thing. In the case of electric utility properties their rate structure is lower for industrial customers than for low-volume domestic consumers, so their revenue loss from an economic downturn may not come from the more profitable part of their business. So we are led to the conclusion that in the case of telephone companies, as compared to electric utilities, the financial risk is less because of the capital structure, but the business risk is greater because of vulnerability of economic downturns. So we are looking at two different types of risk when we talk about the risk considerations involved in actually building a capitalization rate.

Reeves: Clarence, those are good comments and perhaps we can elaborate more upon them later in this conversation. I have the feeling that the whole cap rate problem could bear a great deal more discussion. I also have the feeling what has been said up to now is that the band-of-investment approach to developing a rate of capitalization is the most useful one that we could employ at the present time, and that the market approach may have very little usefulness in valuation process for railroad and utility properties and that there are several other areas of the whole valuation problem that we should begin to explore. Perhaps Coleman Coffey could lead off in taking us down one of these new paths.

Effect of Income Tax on Cost of Capital

Coleman Coffey: One thing I have wondered about a good many times is: What influence on the bond rate does the fact that the interest is tax deductible have? Does the tax deductible status of the interest charges have any real influence on the establishing of the market rate of bonds? Is it really true that the issuing company is willing to pay a 10 percent interest rate on bonds and that the investing public is really asking a lower rate on its common stock investment? If that is true, I would like to know why. And if this is indeed true, is there some role that this apparent contradiction in investment behavior should play in developing our capitalization rate?

Reeves: Well, who would like to wrestle with that bear?

Coffey: Well, it is 5 percent to the issuing corporation. We know that. So should we use the actual net cost of interest in calculating our capitalization rate? And I must say that I really do not know. But this I do know: If we do that, you get a capitalization rate that is more closely related to the one that is actually in use in most taxing jurisdictions, and I have observed that if you use the kind of figures we have been talking about up to now, you get a final capitalization rate in the region of 10 percent. Then if you turn around and take a utility company that is earning $35 million a year, that means by the capitalized earnings approach you have an indicated value for the company of $350 million. But we find the net book value of the same company is $500 million, and we find that the stock-and-debt indicator of value is between $350 and $400 million and then, lo and behold, we find an assessment of $550 million on this property. So my questions come back to this: Does that mean that the capitalization rates that we have been using are incorrect?

Fisher: You are arguing the theoretical question of whether you should use the indicated market rate of return or the net effective rate to the corporation?

Coffey: Yes.

Reeves: Are you not really asking why the buyer is willing to purchase the bond at 10 percent and the stock at 8 percent?

Coffey: Yes, but those are really two different questions, and I would like to have both of them addressed.

Fisher: But what is the difference, Coleman, between taking the market price of a house and saying that the net price is what is going to come back to the seller? I think we are all talking about the gross price or the surface price or initial price or whatever you wish to call it of the cost of debt money. The cost of debt money to you is whatever you are going to have to pay for it on the open market. It is the same as if you are going to buy a piece of real property. You are going to pay out a certain percent for any mortgage money that you get, and this may mean that the net cost to you might be something different from the nominal or gross cost.

Coffey: I agree with you, but does this influence what we are trying to determine here? First, what is the impact of the fact that bond interest is tax deductible? What part does that play in the scenario that we are trying to develop?

Fisher: Well, how about common stock? Isn't it in the same fix? Aren't the corporations paying at the 48 percent tax level on all those earnings beyond a certain minimum amount?

Coffey: No, I do not think that applies to the issue that we are discussing.

McDougall: Excuse me, do I understand your question correctly? Are you trying to determine that point in the financial structure where it is best to stop and cut off the growth in bond indebtedness relative to equity?

Coffey: Not necessarily, I am just wondering whether the fact that the 10 percent interest that you are paying on bonds is tax deductible has a bearing on developing a capitalization rate for the company. And I must confess I really do not know.

Woolery: I will take a crack at that. I think that money is just another commodity or another thing that the company is purchasing and it has a price just like anything else that the company buys. I do not think that there is any argument that would support concern about the tax deductibility of interest anymore than any other expense or any other purchase. So I don't think that you would even be concerned about the company's tax situation in calculating a rate of capitalization. That particular item or consideration should not enter into our calculations. What is the difference between paying interest for money or wages for labor? I don't think there is any.

Coffey: And, of course, the fact that dividends paid by the corporation are not a deductible item in the corporation tax return certainly has to distinguish the equity position as being different from the position of debt.

Woolery: That is right, debt and equity assume different risk-reward positions but I do not think you should tamper with the bond rate simply because interest expense is deductible to the corporation. I do not think that has any bearing on the 10 percent figure as the debt contribution to the band-of-investment method of calculating your capitalization rate.

Coffey: Your direct influence comes by your rating—that is, the classification of rating of your bonds by investing institutions and bond rating firms such as Moody's and Standard & Poor's. For each rating successively higher that a corporation can achieve, there is going to be a corresponding reduction of the interest rate. And the criteria for this rating or at least part of the criteria for this rating is the amount of earnings—that is, the actual net earnings available to pay interest—and that is part of the calculation that actually classifies or determines the interest rate that the corporation is going to pay for its bonded debt. It is my feeling that the issuing company is more willing to pay 10 percent or 12 percent interest on bonds simply because that charge is a tax deductible item.

McCreath: They may be, but their group of equity holders is not. The shareholders are concerned with any higher interest rate that must be paid because the more that goes out to debt, the less that is left to come back to equity. And if it is a tightly regulated company, they can only earn on their historic cost depreciated. They are limited to a certain percent return on that investment and so the stockholder or your equity investor is going to demand his fair share of that return. So therefore, through their investment corporations and through the equity holding groups, there is going to be some pressure to put a limit on the amount of interest that is paid out.

Reeves: The difference between the deductibility of the cost of debt capital and the fact that you cannot deduct the cost of equity—that is, dividends are not tax deductible—will affect the relative attractiveness of the two as investments. But I do not see how it would really affect the point that is being questioned here.

McDougall: I would like to follow up on that by suggesting that the tax effect would be reflected in the relative proportions of debt and equity in the total capital structure and not necessarily in the rate that would be attached to each of these particular components of the capital structure. It is simply the weighting of each in the capital structure of the company that is affected.

McSwain: All the companies want to finance their capital improvements at the lowest possible cost. The interest rate on bonds is going to be influenced by the market because what they are trying to do is attract the money that is available that otherwise could go into savings bonds, savings accounts, government bonds, and almost anything else. The relative return and risk on these particular alternative investments is what is going to govern the interest rate on the bonds issued by a regulated corporation. All money is in competition with all other money and when this type of investment is attractive—that is, it is a good competitor in the market—money will flow into this type of investment. So, I do not see where the tax deductibility feature even plays a part in this particular discussion.

Welch: The value of the property has to be related to the net income after income taxes. In the case of bonded indebtedness since the interest is deductible, you automatically get an after-tax net income out of it, the tax being zero. In the case of equity capital, despite the contention of some of the California county assessors, and I am sure local assessors in other states, you do have to reckon with the fact that the earnings that go to the equity investor or are withheld as undistributed profits are subject to corporation income taxes, usually at both the state and federal levels. These taxes have to be reckoned with, either by deducting them before calculating the net income to be capitalized or by including an income tax component in the capitalization rate. In California, we have chosen to go the latter route—that is, we have included a component for income taxes in the rate of capitalization applied to the income before deducting the income tax. I should point out that there are some problems associated with this approach. Nevertheless, I prefer it over the alternative method of deducting income tax as an expense. But in both instances we are, in effect, removing the income tax consequences before we arrive at the rate that we use in capitalizing net income.

Reeves: The question in this regard, Ron, I believe, boils down to this: If you were capitalizing something other than net income, wouldn't you need to make an adjustment in the rate of capitalization to compensate for the inclusion of the income taxes in the income to be capitalized?

Welch: Yes, you can capitalize the income to equity before deduction of the income taxes, and when you do so, you would apply a higher capitalization rate to a higher income base. Likewise, if you were to use gross revenues as the amount of income to be capitalized, then of course the capitalization rate would have to be further modified to reflect the fact that you are capitalizing a figure higher up in the income stream.

Reeves: But it would not make any real difference whether or not you specifically included the income taxes in the income to be capitalized since you would be making an offsetting adjustment in the capitalization rate.

Welch: I think that is a true statement, and I agree with it.

Market Versus Imbedded Cost of Debt

Reeves: Who would like to raise the next question?

McSwain: I always have a question to raise. One thing, Ron, I would like to go through is the calculation that we talked about earlier when you discussed the interest rate of 10 percent on bonded indebtedness. I would like to ask whether that is a 10 percent interest rate as the current market cost of debt or is that the imbedded rate for debt?

Welch: The current cost of debt.

McSwain: You believe in the current cost?

Welch: Right. I understand why you raise the question of imbedded debt since that is what the regulatory agency commonly considers in setting rates of return.

McSwain: But it seems to me as if you are dealing with an income stream that has been based on the utility's actual cost of money. And if you use something else—that is, if you went to the current cost of money—then under the theory of regulation where you are allowed to earn your expenses plus a reasonable return to the equity holders, you would have to go back and readjust your income stream to take care of the higher interest cost to reflect the higher current cost of debt. So it appears to me that if you are using the actual income stream from the property as it is now situated, you almost have to use the imbedded cost of debt.

Welch: You do not capitalize income after interest deduction; you capitalize income before the deduction of interest.

McSwain: Right.

Welch: I find it very helpful to think in terms of what we actually do in the case of appraising residential properties because that particular appraisal problem is a great deal more familiar to most of us and falls well within the range of our common understanding. My son bought a home some years ago, and it had a mortgage on it at a very favorable interest rate. So he paid considerably more for that property because of the fact he was allowed to assume the low-rate mortgage than he would have paid for the same property if he had paid cash outright or had refinanced the house at the current cost of debt. And our position in California is that the part of the purchase price he paid for the favorable low-cost mortgage was really not part of the property value for tax purposes. The difference between what he paid for the loan and the total price is the amount that he actually paid for the house. But what he paid for the house was something less than the stated total purchase price in that transaction. I think it is the same way with imbedded debt.

McSwain: Well, I am not sure that I agree because in one case you are dealing with a regulated company, and in the other situation you are dealing in the free market price. I think that is the real difference. I think what really happens in this situation is this: If the imbedded cost of capital is 6.5 percent and the current cost of debt is 10 percent and you were to buy that company, you certainly would not pay off the 6.5 percent debt and refinance it with 10 percent money. Also, I do not think the regulatory commission would allow you to load that additional 3.5 percent on the consumer. So I think that where you are dealing with the regulated income stream, you have to consider the actual imbedded debt structure and its cost rather than the current cost of debt. I know in considering this argument that Dr. Ring used to hold the position that you just mentioned here, but now it is my opinion that perhaps Dr. Ring is beginning to look at it from the other point of view.

Fisher: I guess you have been talking to him, Bob.

Oldman: I think at this point Bob is getting back to rate regulation and is leaving the field of property taxation and that we have to come back again to what we are trying to do with the valuations that we are talking about. I would agree with Bob if what he was saying is that if you make a property tax valuation

44

using current cost of debt, which is quite different from the imbedded cost of debt, then the valuations will be sufficiently different so that the property tax will be quite a bit higher under one set of circumstances than under the other. Now the property tax will immediately affect the rate regulators, and if it increases, they will allow an increase in the income stream. That would be quite proper, and it would seem to me that at the same time the rate regulator would be looking at the actual income stream for purposes of setting of rates for the next year and would be looking at the imbedded costs and not the current costs. As long as we keep separate our willingness to compute the value of the company's property for property tax purposes and are willing to do that differently than using the values derived from the actual income stream for rate-making purposes, then there are no real inconsistencies involved, and the impact on the income stream of the higher-than-otherwise property tax would be a real impact, but a proper impact considering the relation of the utility property values to all other property values within the particular taxing jurisdiction. And unless you are willing to go further than California is willing to go, and Ron is willing to go, you would have to say that the property tax should reach into the area of intangible values. Most states do not do this or if they do it, they do it by another route. Unless you are willing to assess and tax intangible values wherever you find them, then it seems to me you have to do exactly what Ron Welch said—that is, if you are going to be consistent in your administration of the property tax. I don't see how you can argue with that particular point of view. If you can, then I am completely misunderstanding what is happening here.

McSwain: No, I think we lose sight of the fundamental difference here, and that is we are dealing with property that is subject to regulation. I think the fact that it is subject to regulation affects its value, and I think you have to recognize that whenever you apply the appraisal process.

Welch: I would not differ with that particular statement.

Regulation and Valuation

McSwain: I think here we are talking about a regulated company, and the regulatory commission, under the Hope Natural Gas Company case and several other cases of the same type, says that the utility is permitted to earn its expenses—that is, its interest, operating expense—and be allowed a fair rate of return for its equity owners. The regulatory commission permits a utility to earn on the basis of imbedded debt, and the rate structure for that company is based upon its costs for imbedded debt and an allowable rate of return to the equity holders. Now, if I bought that company, all I could expect out of it would be the current rates set by the regulatory commission—and those rates would be based on imbedded costs—and I would not be willing to pay any more for it than would be reflected by that particular method of capitalization. If I use current cost of debt and assume that the income stream remains the same, my interest costs would go up, the money left for the equity holders would go way down. Hence, the return to equity would go down or I would pay a whole lot less for the company, and I do not think that would be the case. I think the situation would be that I would get substantially the same income stream that the company is receiving now.

Oldman: Under certain circumstances that's a very effective argument from the point of view of the companies, but I don't see why the property tax administrator or the courts would have to rule on the difference. It seems to me what you have done is outline with great skill exactly how the representative of the company would argue this case.

McSwain: The company representatives argue exactly the opposite case.

Welch: Exactly.

McSwain: Because if you go the other way, it produces a much lower valuation than if you go the way of using imbedded debt costs in the construction of your capitalization rate.

Oldman: In this case, because of the present relationship of current rates and past rates, that is true. But in another period of history, that could be the reverse.

Woolery: I would like to raise a question for the panel, which I think is germane to Bob's point. We presume that the regulatory agency is set up as a competitor in the absence of free-market competition. Implicit in Bob McSwain's remarks is the assumption that the regulatory body is an unfair competitor, and as a result we should be valuing regulated property lower than we value property that operates in a free-market economy. If Bob McSwain's remarks are true, is there any validity for this particular premise?

Martin: Lower in relationship to what?

Woolery: The free market without rate regulation. Are regulatory bodies fair competition for regulated companies? And if they are not fair, then do we have to reduce the value of the companies they regulate so they will be comparable in property value to unregulated properties that are in the tax base?

Welch: I think that certainly must be true with respect to the use of original cost less depreciation as distinguished from reproduction cost less depreciation, and I doubt there would be any difference of opinion among the practitioners here as to which of those is the proper basis for valuation where the utility commission uses the historical cost rate base. Certainly they are getting a much lower rate of return than they would get if they were unregulated and operating in a market that would support reproduction cost less depreciation.

Reeves: You're saying that Arlo's point would be automatically taken care of by the differences in cap rate for industries of this nature. Is that right?

Welch: No. I think it is taken care of in the income amount to be capitalized. Theoretically, equally risky income streams should receive the same rate of capitalization. Generally, the regulated utility companies have a fairly low rate of risk, and that is the reason we capitalize their income stream at a comparatively low capitalization rate. And, of course, the income stream is much less for those companies that are regulated on historic cost less depreciation than the income would be if they were regulated on the basis of reproduction cost less depreciation.

Woolery: This is really a two-part question, and the second part is, if what you say is correct, what would be the impact of Public Law 94-210 when you come to the problem of equalizing railroad valuation with the valuation of all other commercial and industrial property? Aren't we going to be looking at two different yardsticks employed to measure equalization levels?

Welch: That is a heresy that I have heard too often, and I don't think you are advancing it with a great deal of sincerity, Arlo. The equality relationship that we are looking for is measured by the assessment level as related to the actual market value, and market value always has to be the value arrived at subject to those institutional forces that have been established legally and then enforced. Rate regulation is one of those legal restraints that must be recognized. Certainly the market recognizes it, and therefore, the assessor has to recognize it.

Bonbright: Of course. On the other hand, the commissions are likely to protect the regulated company against other competitors. The Federal Communication Commission has very much offended the Bell System by permitting a significant degree of competition.

Martin: Arlo, I am in accord with what Ron said, but I would add—and this goes for corporations that are not in the legal sense affected by the public interest—that there are various kinds of regulations, income tax regulations, safety regulations, labor relations regulations, and a horde of other kinds of regulations that apply to industrial corporations generally, to mining companies, and all of the rest of them.

Of course, rate regulation is a brand of regulation that is aimed more point-edly at the utility type operations. It is in one sense of the word, but not 100 percent in practice, additional to the regulations that are placed on other types of corporations. But regulation of utilities is one thing that government has developed into sort of a fine art, although not very fine. I would suggest to you that among other things, the regulation of public utility rates is pretty crude sometimes. I do not think that in most states we do get anything approaching the precision that our friend McSwain suggested here when he was formulating his generalization. It was a good generalization, but not really true to life be-cause there is a whale of a lot of friction here as there is in all other corporate regulations.

McSwain: You know, this whole question of regulation and its effect on value gets right down to the basic unit. For instance, I use this example quite a bit: This is, say, a street in Montgomery, Alabama, and this is a lot—125' × 200'—on a corner of that street. We have a real strict zoning commission, and that zoning commission has zoned that lot R-125s, which means the only use that lot could be put to is for single-family residential purposes. That lot would sell for about $15,000. If the zoning commission lifted the restriction and zoned it R-125m, it could be used for multi-family residential purposes. There would be a higher density use for that particular land. On that same property you could put a three-unit townhouse. Then that same lot would sell for $25,000. It is located in the same place, it is the same size, and the same everything else. The only thing that has changed is the governmental restriction imposed on that property. If we go one more step and say that C-1 zoning had been allowed on that particular property, back before the shortage of oil and gas, Pure Oil Com-pany or Texaco or any of your major oil companies would have paid $100,000 for that same lot. In that case, as I said before, it is the same lot, same location, same everything except the regulatory control on the use to which it could be put. I think that clearly shows that governmental restrictions affect value, and I could show you hundreds of examples just like this.

Welch: I do not think there would be any disagreement around the table on that.

Martin: No, I think that that applies to public utility properties also.

McSwain: I think for the same reason that restrictions affect the value of let's say, railroads. Not only are they subject to many types of regulation, but they are also subject to competition, from pipelines, trucks, and barge lines. If all of a sudden all the restrictions were removed from the railroad industry—instead of having a ten-man crew when they needed three people, instead of a crew work-ing three hours and stopping and exchanging with another crew, they were allowed to use good economic labor practices—and if they were allowed to abandon unprofitable lines and charge competitive rates, I think our railroads would be much more valuable than they are today.

Reeves: But, in any case, for valuing or for tax purposes, you are trying to determine the value that property has in the use that is permitted, or that is likely to be permitted with some impact for that deviant possibility that might conceivably be permitted. You must take all those things into consideration and that brings us back to the fundamental question, does the value estimate produced by capitalization of income actually take all of these variables and possibilities into full consideration?

McSwain: If everything is considered, it seems to me as if it would because those restrictions would limit income, and so you have automatically taken them into consideration.

Reeves: I take it then that you and Ron would be in pretty complete agreement on this particular issue.

Welch: I think mostly we would be, although it is possible there would still be a difference in how we view the handling of funded debt. I would use the current cost of capital rather than the historical or so-called imbedded cost of capital.

McSwain: But if I use current cost, I would have to go back and adjust my income stream.

Welch: But you see the utility commission is going to do that.

McSwain: But I maintain the utility commission is not going to make them use the current cost of debt.

Welch: I agree, the utility commission is going to use the imbedded cost, so that is the income you forecast. But we are going to capitalize income before deduction of interest.

McSwain: But your interest will be included in your cap rate.

Fisher: But one is a rate or regulatory control attitude and one is a market value consideration.

McSwain: If you were buying this railroad, would you go out and pay off your 6.5 percent money with 10 percent money? You would not do it. You would retain your 6.5 percent.

Coffey: But you could go to the marketplace and pick up that debt at a discounted rate.

Oldman: But there is a problem of up and down. We have been talking only about periods when the imbedded rates are much lower than the current rates, but historically the reverse has happened just as frequently, and as soon as you reverse the situation, then you cannot conceive of a buyer coming in without refinancing. That is the first thing he would do subject to any legal restrictions on his being able to refund the debt. You would not refinance up; you would refinance down to the extent that the regulatory body permits. I think that from the point of view of the public interest, as a matter of managing the property tax, one ought to be fair both up and down and employ the current cost of debt in cap rate calculations. Then the way in which you allocate the property tax liabilities among all property taxpayers should be a fair one. In fact, in order to be fair to all property taxpayers, you would have to do that. Now that may impose a burden on the utility rate makers in that they would have to take into account this change that you make, meaning that sometimes you would be putting on a property tax that would be higher if you were using imbedded cost and at other times it would be lower. And it would be the rate maker's function to follow the actual property tax in establishing his rates. But the property tax administrator ought to look at the current cost as the way of doing his job, and while I may have had things backward before in saying what your view would have as an impact today, it is equally true to say exactly the opposite. Why are you so zealous on behalf of the taxpayers rather than pursuing a view that gives a higher property tax base in a situation that is not justified in light of what is happening with other taxpayers? And again, it seems to me that . . .

McSwain: Well, let me interrupt. The other taxpayers being in a free marketplace are at liberty to adjust upward or downward without going before the regulatory commission.

Oldman: But, as Ron pointed out with his son's house, the people in the market cannot really adjust up and down since they are subject to institutional restrictions such as mortgages.

McSwain: But I think there you are dealing with a situation that is isolated to a certain extent. In our area we have situations of houses in which you can get low-cost money, perhaps 6 percent interest. But then the down payment is so large that people will pay a whole lot less for those places because the only thing they are really interested in is the size of the monthly payment and how much they are going to put down. So, I think the motive there might be a little different from a situation someplace else. If you have two houses side by side, this house might be a better buy from an economic standpoint. You would pay less interest but more of a down payment and a shorter mortgage time. The second house would cost more, but they might not have to put any money down or maybe only a couple of hundred dollars down. The monthly payments would be a lot more than on the first house, but they are willing to make those payments.

Oldman: But really the only relevant question in that case, assuming the two houses are identical as you postulated, is should they pay the same property tax or a different property tax when they have these widely different financial arrangements? Now as a property tax administrator, it seems to me that they should pay exactly the same property tax. The fact that they paid different purchase prices, which were determined by the financial terms of the sale, has nothing whatsoever to do with the amount that should be collected as property tax. Now, if we carry that same principle over to utilities, you are forced really to Ron's view that the current cost of debt should be used in calculating a band-of-interest capitalization rate.

Woolery: I would like to ask a question, Bob. How is this any different from a sandwich lease on an income property where you value the leased fee interest and the leasehold interest? As far as I can see, the low-cost imbedded debt is the equivalent to the sandwich lease portion that you would not value as part of the leased fee interest. It is not really part of the property itself; it is a value that attaches to the terms of the lease. That particular interest is not taxable under the property tax statutes of many of our states. I think you have to come back to Ron's position that you must use current cost of debt. I think that that decision is inescapable.

McSwain: But in some cases you can sell the leasehold interest. It does have a value.

Oldman: Of course. But the real question remains, is it subject to the property tax and, if so, on what basis?

McSwain: I think the whole question boils down to regulation, and I can't get away from the idea that imbedded cost of debt is the only thing that makes sense. I think that we just about got several former advocates turned around on that, and they were just like Ron when it came to this topic.

Woolery: Well, I think they were in good company.

Franzman: Without prolonging this particular phase of our discussion, I have a couple of observations I would like to throw in for what they are worth. In talking about the two houses with different mortgage terms, I think we have been talking about the difference between price and value, and I think we all acknowledge that there is a significant difference between these two words and the meanings they carry. Secondly, if Bob McSwain's assumptions about imbedded debt are correct and he owns that corner lot about which he drew the diagram and the zoning were changed from R-125s with the attendant $15,000 value on that lot to C-1 zoning at $100,000, is he going to consider the imbedded cost of debt when calculating the return on that investment, or is he going to look at alternative market data for the value, not price, of that particular lot?

Reeves: We have gotten somewhat far afield in our discussion in pursuit of the cap rate. Shall we try to get back to that?

Coffey: It appears to me from Bob McSwain's illustration and what we know about most going concern electric companies that the state of California is now valuing at something less than book value for property tax purposes?

Martin: So what?

Coffey: Well, that is all right, but the way that Bob suggests would result in values closer to those established by a regulatory body.

McSwain: I think now, because of regulatory lag, most of our valuations for property tax purposes are below the net book figure because the commissions are tied up in politics more than anything else, and the incomes they are allowing these utilities to earn are not sufficient. So I find, in my appraisals, that the final conclusion of value is sometimes below net book.

Value as Defined by Statutes

Bonbright: I would like to ask a simple question at this point. To what extent, if at all, is the measure of value for such problems as we are now discussing predetermined, or at least influenced, by the phrasing of the statutes?

McSwain: Our statutes in Alabama just say market value, so that is it.

Welch: That is pretty characteristic of the laws around the country. Wisconsin has a little broader law than just the market value requirement. As I recall it, Wisconsin law says that you are to value all utility property including intangibles, whereas most states simply apply to utilities the same criteria of taxability as applies to all other property.

McSwain: Clarence, doesn't the Florida law apply something like nine different criteria of value?

Brasfield: The Florida constitution provides for valuation at just value, and that has been interpreted by the courts to be equivalent to fair market value, which incorporates the informed willing buyer/willing seller concepts. But the statute does point to eight different criteria that must be considered in arriving at just value. That is the distinction in Florida.

McSwain: I should state that it is Florida and not Georgia that makes that kind of an application.

Bonbright: How many states would value the building of the New York Stock Exchange at any substantial amount in view of the fact that it is unique, special purpose property and could hardly be sold to any other buyer for any other use? How do we reconcile this concept with a recent Wisconsin case in which the courts substantially reduced the valuation of a golf course on the grounds that the course could not be sold to anybody else?

Welch: I do not think very many places would support that kind of a conclusion. As long as the owner is a going concern, you must make the assumption that the property would be purchased by someone who would make the same general use of the property as the owner and that it would be continued in the operation that it is in. Your buyer would be clearly hypothetical. The New York Stock Exchange does not have to sell its building to the American Stock Exchange or any other named exchange. It could sell the building to X Stock Exchange or to itself.

Bonbright: Then aren't you presuming the existence of a stock exchange that may never actually exist?

Welch: No. I don't know why you say it wouldn't exist. I think that if the New York Stock Exchange should decide for some peculiar reason that it does not wish to continue in existence, somebody else would conjure up a new stock exchange and buy the building from them. I think that is what assessors would generally say.

McSwain: Well, in generally accepted appraisal practice, would you not value the land and then determine whether there were any uses for the building?

Welch: But not an alternative use. It would have to be the same use, and it would be the same way with the golf course. I cannot imagine there being fewer golf courses required. I think that golf courses would go out of existence for reasons other than loss of business. In fact, I think if one were on the market, someone would pick it up and run it as a golf course if there were no more profitable uses. So I don't believe that those Wisconsin decisions have much validity or vitality.

Oldman: There is another way of looking at that same problem. What is generally assumed in dealing with the unique situations, be it a stock exchange building or a golf course in an area that can only support one golf course, is that the owner is excluded from consideration in deciding upon the market value because of the desire to get away from subjective value. But it seems to me there is no reason in principle why we have to exclude the owner from the market. It may well happen that there is only one person in the market and that is the present owner, and maybe we shouldn't be using the maximum value that the present owner would be willing to put into the property. But we ought to use, at least as a minimum, the cost of building the facilities, which is the way most of these cases do come out in the end. What is never clear is how the courts reach their results. But they could reach their decisions very easily by concluding that we should not exclude the owner himself from the market as long as he is actually using the property for the purposes for which it was designed. Then you can get very easily to the natural result.

Bonbright: While I have the chance, could I ask the question? What is the meaning of the word *fair* when we insert that word in front of "market value"? Say a property has a market value of $10 million, and we agree on that, but we won't accept that figure because it is an *unfair* market value. I think we are unwise to talk in terms of "fair" or "unfair" as modifiers relating to market value. If we want market value, let's get to the market value. "Fair" or "unfair," it is generally what the property will bring in the marketplace.

Oldman: I guess I have always assumed that fair in the legal sense meant fair procedures and access to information.

Bonbright: Then what you are saying is that we are setting the stage for a fair, that is unbiased, *estimate* of "actual market value."

Oldman: Yes, that is what I always thought. But "fair" is a redundancy of the type that lawyers often like to insert into legal documents.

Reeves: I should caution Professor Oldman that he is being quoted here and that all of this is being taped.

Bonbright: But you would not find a decision saying, in effect, that this property has an actual value of $10 million, but that for tax purposes it must be valued at only $8 million, since a $10 million valuation is unfairly large. Oh yes, it could be sold for $10 million, but that would be an *unfair* price.

Oldman: I can't think of any case where that happens, but I suppose it could. It would just be a way of obscuring the issue when the valuer was in doubt about something such as a favorable lease that might result in a price of $10 million. But it is not fair to tax this property at $10 million when all other similar properties are being taxed at only $8 million, and that kind of reasoning I could understand. I think this happens when we fail to make explicit our hidden assumptions about the meaning of value or the definition of taxable property.

Woolery: Well, I have always heard that when you talk about "fair market" value, you are talking about a market that is neither very good or very bad, but just a "fair market," a normal or typical market. What they have really done by inserting the word fair is caution the appraiser to value the property in terms of what is typical at the time of the valuation and not value it as if the market were better or worse than the one prevailing on the date of the appraisal. I think we should really get back to Mr. Bonbright's initial point if we are going to talk about market value. Let's call it that and not try to qualify it with a whole host of adjectives like "fair" or "true" or the many other things we are inclined to inject prior to stating what we are really looking for in the first place.

Welch: That makes good sense. Of course, there have been instances, even in court decisions where it has been held that "normal value" was quite different from what you could sell the property for now—it was much higher. That is a very dangerous concept. I think "fair market" value has the same inherent dangers in it. But I must say that in California we have inserted the term "fair market value" into our constitution. I suppose that our excuse was that it sounds better. Who could object to being assessed at *fair* market value?

Reeves: Well, isn't it true that if you are drafting legislation, it is wise to stay away from adjectives such as "fair" and "normal"?

Oldman: While we are on that topic, it might be useful to get the sense of the group here as to whether or not the view that I find more and more widely expressed may be one of the troubles with this whole valuation area. This view is that the lawyers have not drafted much more detailed laws to explain exactly what they mean by *value*. If a lot of this wording were straightened out, a lot of the problems that we now have would vanish. I have never been able to see how I would write the statute to say other than "estimated market value" and to add anything more than would be useful as a guide for experts. I am getting a little weary of constantly being accused of being part of a system that refuses to spell out exactly what it means. I would like to get some sense as to whether this group thinks there is a way that would make more sense than market value when inserted into the statutes or constitutions of the states.

Reeves: I don't believe your accusers understand the lawyers and the judicial concept.

McSwain: In most situations in which I have been involved, the fewer words that we can use the better, and that is what we try to do. It seems to me every-time you add a word to something, you add problems, and it has always been my recommendation that all you should say is "all utility property shall be appraised on the basis of market value," and let it go at that. I think then that we are better off than if we try to explain it.

Oldman: You don't think that the property tax statutes should get as long as the federal Internal Revenue Code?

McSwain: No, but speaking of court decisions, we had a real interesting case a few years ago involving Dr. Martin as a witness. We had a judge who was re-nowned the country over. His name was Judge Walter Jones, and the case involved a railroad valuation. There was not much law at that time on railroad valuations, and everybody knew that Judge Jones was really going to set down the guidelines. Dr. Martin and several others were witnesses, and I guess we had a stack of letters four feet high from people all over the country saying that when the decision comes out, be sure to send them a copy and that whatever charge you want to put for this service, just bill us and we will send you the money. Of course, everybody was anticipating something great from Judge Jones's decision, but when it came out, Judge Jones said: "The court finds the value of the Southern Railway to be $22 million"—signed Walter J. Jones, Judge. And that is the decision he handed down. He did not want to get involved in the detail of appraising railroads.

Reeves: Well, is there any further comment on Ollie's question about the sense of this group on the proper terminology or definition of market value? Would more language actually help property tax statutes?

Woolery: I would like to comment. I certainly like the wording Ollie has men-tioned, but I would like to ask, isn't it generally true in law that the longer the opinion, the more frequently there is a basis for appeal? Wouldn't the opinion that Jones wrote be very difficult to appeal?

Oldman: Well, it is axiomatic. Of course, like all axioms, there are exceptions. The question, I suppose, is that unlike a legal opinion a statute that is to be an aegis must be a little more carefully done and must involve more time and effort than a judge could put into an opinion. If we all put our heads together long enough in a LILP seminar, could we come up with a few more words of statutory language that would make life easier for the people who have to administer the property tax statutes?

Welch: I think we can. In California we had a very antiquated statutory definition of taxable value. So when we were told by the legislature that we had to write rules, we wrote some rules, and the second rule that we wrote was a definition of value. We wrote it in terms not dissimilar from those that appear in the AIREA handbooks and other textbooks. We defined it in terms of the buyer and the seller having knowledge of the property and the buyer having the opportunity to learn all of the uses of the property, and then picked up some language from California court decisions, and we found it to be very helpful. We had assessors saying, seemingly in all seriousness, that value was all sorts of things that no self-respecting appraiser would ever say it was, such as "the value is 50 percent of what a property sells for." I think you can write a definition that follows generally the literature in the field. I would not write it in the constitution, I suppose, because you really do not need to—you can cover that with the statutes and the rules and regulations—and I don't see any harm in that as long as you write it with some care.

Oldman: In the event that you use that language, though, and employ it literally, say, in a favorable or unfavorable lease situation for instance, some interesting questions are raised. I asked some of my students to do this on an examination about a month ago. I simply posed the question in terms of valuing property that was encumbered by an unfavorable lease. We had not discussed it in class up to that point, so I really gave the class a chance to be creative in the examination. And I was amazed at the high percentage of the class who said while it is quite clear that a favorable lease will add to the value of the property on an open market, the owner would be able to sell the property for more money, which would indicate more ability to pay, and therefore let's tax him on the actual selling price with the favorable lease. That was typical of the answers we received to that particular question in the examination. So my question is: How do you write your definition of value so that kind of thing would not crop up, and it would be obvious to any reader of the language that you had not intended to include some of these extraneous values that may add to or diminish the real value because of a contract or lease?

Welch: You are really getting to what you are valuing rather than what is the taxable property's value. There is no question about the fact that the property is worth less if it is encumbered by an adverse lease. But that is not the property you are supposed to be valuing.

Oldman: That is exactly the problem. So I guess the question then is whether or not, in giving a statement in a constitution or a statute, the tax should be on a fair market value of the property. The question then comes back to how far you go in defining property as compared to how far you go in defining value. And what you said is that you have found it useful to add the willing buyer/willing seller type of valuation language right in the law to make sure that the people administering the law do not get off on tangents. What I am saying is that it may be useful to give some kind of a guideline as to the meaning of property for property tax purposes to show that it is not the same as property under general law purposes for wills, estates, and other things. Most property tax laws are lacking in definitions of that kind. So maybe we have helped each other answer that question in terms of deciding that there is room for a few words to be added in the current definitions contained in our statutes.

Fisher: The property itself has not changed in value. It is just the lessees' and lessors' interests that have had shifts in relative values because of favorable and unfavorable leases. The property itself is just the same.

Oldman: The property that is subject to the tax is just the same, providing you describe it in a certain way. The lessees' and lessors' interests in the lease are going to cancel each other out.

Fisher: Well, you are right back to the bundle-of-sticks concept. There is always 100 percent in the total bundle of sticks, but the value of the individual sticks may vary.

Oldman: But that has to be defined in a fairly precise way to make sure your total bundle includes what might be a negative value. That would be true in the case of the lessee who had an unfavorable lease. He would be willing to pay something to get out of the lease and would have a negative value in the bundle of rights. That is just as much a part of the bundle as a favorable lease is in the hands of the owner of the equity.

Harriss: There is another observation that is relevant here, and that is the "obligation to serve." A railroad, for instance, must maintain a certain level of service. To do so, it must maintain lines in use that are not capable of generating enough revenue tocover the cost of operation of that line. If they are going to stay in business as an operating railroad, they have obligations to serve that really constitute, under certain conditions, negative values. The total railroad trackage into Grand Central Station in New York City (under Park Avenue) really has a negative value. The roads have been losing money for years. The tracks with the legal compulsion to provide rail service really constitute a drain on the entire railroad system. The companies continue to provide service, but at a loss. They cannot end the operation and use the property for purposes that might yield positive income.[c]

Reeves: Negative value of this type would be different from an adverse lease wouldn't it, in that you could never buy yourself out of it?

Oldman: What you are getting down to is this: When you are valuing the total unit of which a part has a negative value, that part should be subtracted from the total.

Reeves: That automatically occurs, we would assume, in the application of any reasonable assessment approach.

Franzman: I would like to make an observation that we find an obsolescence of statute as well as an obsolescence of property itself. There is often a great deal of archaic language in statutes that should be removed, but it is such a laborious and time-consuming process, it seldom gets done, so we carry on things like reporting requirements that generate information that is no longer necessary. Oftentimes, this brings you to the point where you ignore some things that are actually included in the statutory requirements. For instance, in the Arizona statutes the section applying to the taxation of express companies uses this language in one place: "... less the amount paid to railroads for transporting express." And this has been amended now to exclude the payments for air express. Of course, airplanes were not even considered as express carriers at the time the statute was written. So you change the entire concept of the statute by including a word that might well have been omitted in the first place.

Oldman: Of course, the inclusion of that word helps supply an interpretation of the language that is extremely narrow. That leads to the kind of result you describe, but I should point out that it is not an inevitable result.

Franzman: I think it is to the narrowness of interpretation that I'm objecting.

Oldman: But it also happens to supply a method of interpreting language that is extremely narrow and then leads to the kind of result you have now described. But that is not an inevitable result of such statutory language and the battle of interpretation, of course, is a very important and continuous battle. On this property tax language, the most common feature of the statute is to say that it applies to real property and let it go at that, and then leave it up to the other laws of the state to define *real property*. And what we are talking about here is

---

[c]See Appendix E.

that real property should have a definition that is different from all other definitions of general real property.

Woolery: Suppose we were to set forth a beginning definition such as this: "That estimate of the value of property rights that is derived through the use of standard appraisal methods and techniques."

Oldman: Then the problem becomes one of saying which property rights. Are you going to tax all property rights?

Woolery: That is where I would start.

Oldman: But experience tells us that all states have retreated from that by eliminating taxation of most intangible property rights. So then the question becomes one of what are the things you are going to cut out before you decide this is my base for applying the property tax—that is, I want the property tax to apply to this group of property rights. It is important to identify that group of property rights that we wish to use for property tax purposes. It is something that we ought to do, which up to now has been done very slowly and very laboriously by the courts and quite inconsistently from time to time with a great deal of variation from one state to another. There is really no obvious reason why there should be a difference from one state to another. And that is, it seems to me, an effort that would be worth putting some resources into. These are things that really have not been faced up to in a wholehearted fashion so far as I know. Professor Bonbright tackled these problems some years ago, and that was a first and adequate effort at that particular time. But since then, the whole world of property rights has become so much more complex and there have been so many other kinds of mechanisms that have been introduced into combining and refining the property interests that we have to reexamine those things to determine which are proper subjects for the property tax. This is not really being done except erratically by the courts as problems on the margin keep coming up. If it is not done by the courts, it is done by the property tax administrators as they interpret problems and cases from time to time. I, at least, do not have any systematic picture or concept of what ought to be included in all of this. I would hope that some of you have been working on these things and know what the problems are that might help us identify the kind of things that we ought to be worrying about in trying to get a handle on this. What we need to do, of course, is bring some order out of this chaos and the question is how do you go about doing it?

Franzman: I might observe that having more judges who have read Bonbright's two volumes sometime during their law school studies would be of some help in this problem.

Oldman: I am prepared to state here that there is at least one law school in which they do get some excerpts from Bonbright as part of their law school training. I would expand that comment to say that more assessors who have read Bonbright would also be of help in the administration of our property tax statutes. I have been amazed as I have gone around the country at the number of people who are actually engaged in valuation operations who have never heard of the two volumes written by Bonbright. I must say I found this omission to be absolutely shocking. But that means there are places in this world where you can study valuation and appraisal without ever being exposed to those particular volumes. It is hard for me to see how that can take place if we are to teach anything that is really understandable in the field of valuation.

Rationale of the Property Tax

Bonbright: By the way, so far in the discussion about the property tax, I have not heard any discussion, and there may be good reason for that, as to whether the very meaning of value and perhaps the proper method of valuation ought to be predetermined by the rationale of the property tax itself. For example, insofar as the property tax is justified on the ground that it costs the government more to supply its services to the more valuable property, is it possible to determine the proper meaning of value and the proper method of valuation in terms of the property tax itself? That is, properties that require greater services from the government maybe should be taxed based on higher valuations than properties that require less costly services.

Reeves: Dr. Bonbright, wouldn't that particular problem address itself not to the valuation but to the rate applied to the value? If you want to distinguish different types of property and tax them more nearly in relationship to the cost of service, then wouldn't you need to classify the property and apply different rates to different classes? This would divorce the valuation process from the true taxation process, and from an ad valorem tax administrator's point of view, he would not be concerned about the kind of effort or investment that government put into protecting the property of a private taxpayer.

Bonbright: You may well be right.

McSwain: In Alabama we have fixed rates, and we have one county in which a taxpayer, a major utility, is paying between 90 percent and 91 percent of the total property taxes paid in that entire county. They have a facility worth about $600 million and pay over 90 percent of the total property taxes in that county, but they do not require any major services from the county government. They have their own private security force. The facility is highly automated so there are few employees who generate requirements for personal service from various levels of government. It is a nuclear power plant, and now they are talking about spending $4 billion more in that same county, which would mean about $1.5 billion more in assessed valuation, and by law the tax rate will remain the same.

Franzman: I think what Bob McSwain has just mentioned underscores some of the new problems that were in the list of topics that we were going to talk about in this particular conversation. This is true in many states where one small subdivision or jurisdiction has a great concentration of wealth within its boundaries, and this situation will become more commonplace as we have more nuclear power plants built. I think that the distribution of revenues from installations of this type constitutes a political problem that will have to be solved, and the solution will undoubtedly affect the actions of the tax administrators. I don't think that an acceptable solution has been achieved by anybody up to this time.

McSwain: It is pure human nature; the haves want to keep what they have and the have-nots would like to get a share.

Franzman: Going on further with our thoughts about, for example, nuclear installations, and the large amount of tax paid for the small benefit of public services received, you may have to look beyond that particular argument in favor of lower property tax to consider the impact of the plant's presence on all of the surrounding properties. If the installation of a nuclear generator of this type means that all land for maybe a five-mile radius around it is not going to be used to its full potential, then there is value loss for that entire land area. Perhaps part of the value loss in that land area has to be considered when you are looking at the value of the nuclear plant and the benefit it demands. But to the extent that the presence of a nuclear plant has an impact on the surrounding area, either in development or lack of development, then in the aggregate we may see a greater or lesser development in the area and thereby a greater or lesser development in the tax base in that vicinity than we might normally see. So the question then becomes one of effect on total value within the larger area. Does the presence of a nuclear generating plant stimulate development or inhibit development, and through these mechanisms, what effect does it really have on the total tax base of the entire jurisdiction? Maybe this is a basis for differential assessment ratios or differential tax rates based upon the concept of service.

Reeves: Do I sense from the foregoing remarks that around this table there is a consensus that we are coming to a greater use of differential assessment ratios or what we call classified property tax systems and that most that are engaged in the valuation of property would say that the differential ought to be in the rate and that valuation ought to be the valuation at market value as Dr. Bonbright defined it? It ought to be market value and not something else that we call fair market value or some kind of a modified market value. So that brings us back to the pure problem of defining *market value*, or do I take it from your remarks, Seth, that you are saying the differential valuations are justifiable?

Fleming: I think what we are talking about is differential assessment and not differential valuation. Our goal is always to find market value, and then in certain states, there are classified property tax systems that allow you to put a different assessment ratio against the market value for property tax purposes. In effect, this comes down to taxing at a different rate because when you take the total tax paid as a percentage of the market value, you have effectively changed the tax rate through the mechanism of changing the assessment ratio. Of course, all of these things could change in the wake of Public Law 94-210, the Railroad Revitalization and Regulatory Reform Act. This law specifically prohibits the assessment of railroad property at a rate substantially higher than other commercial and industrial property or the taxation of railroad property at a rate that is different from that applied to the commercial and industrial property within a given jurisdiction. So all of this discussion may be passé with the coming of Public Law 94-210.[d]

Coffey: I would like to bring us back to the problem that we are really addressing in this conversation, and this is the problem of valuation. Many states have in their tax statutes language similar to Kentucky's, at least insofar as railroad property is concerned, which implies some additional value. In Kentucky we call it the franchise value, or the added value, which is something over and above the value of the tangible or physical assets of the company. Also in Kentucky there is an exemption for some public service companies from our state license tax and local occupational taxes. So going along with the requirements of Public Law 94-210, if we are going to treat the railroads the same as other property in the commercial and industrial area for property tax purposes, we may have to subject them to all these other taxes that other companies are paying as a matter of equity.

Welch: There is nothing in the federal law that would prohibit taxing railroads at a lower rate than the other commercial and industrial properties.

McSwain: I think that South Carolina has a classification system where the assessment ratio on railroads is less than the assessment ratio on commercial and industrial property.

Welch: That certainly is not in violation of the federal law, but I thought what Mr. Coffey was addressing was the question of raising the taxes on railroads and

---

[d]See Appendix D.

imposing taxes from which they are now exempt in order to put them on an equal basis with other commercial and industrial property. I think what you are really talking about here is whether these other taxes must be taken into account in deciding whether the taxes on railroad properties are heavier for each dollar of value than the taxes on other types of commerical and industrial property.

Capitalization Rate Components

Reeves: I think we should get back on the track and talk about some of the things that we started out talking about in the first place. Maybe the calculation of capitalization rates and continuing disucussion on the band-of-investment approach and how the capital structure should be handled with the various rates and the market data approach to valuation. Are there some other problems that relate strictly to the capitalization rate?

Welch: I would like to hear some discussion on the proper components of the capitalization rate.

Reeves: This is a part of what I had in mind.

Welch: I keep coming back to what we do in California, and I am getting a little tired of saying what we do in California—and I am sure you are getting tired of hearing it, too—but anyway this is what we do in California: We do include an income tax component in our capitalization rate and we use the formula that appears in the Western States Association of Tax Administrators Utility and Railroad Valuation Report of 1971. The formula also appears in an article that I wrote way back in 1955 and that Jim Martin mentioned earlier. We do capitalize income before depreciation, and we do include a component for depreciation in the capitalization rate. I am not sure we are putting in the right factor since we use the sinking-fund method of calculating depreciation, and I must say I don't know whether that is right or not. Don Fisher, do you have any thoughts on that?

Fisher: Both from a logical standpoint and from a practical standpoint, I think that capitalization ought to be prior to depreciation so that depreciation becomes a function of value rather than a function of some book or historical cost. As far as capitalizing before or after federal income tax, I think that the IRS Code defies any rational conclusion because you have the deferred federal income tax wrapped up in the whole thing, plus the variable rate tax depending upon how much capital gain you have, so I guess you could plug in the statutory 48 percent rate and just assume that it applies across the board. However, when you get to the question of whether you use straight-line or sinking-fund depreciation, you are right back to the philosophy you adopt in the income approach.

If you are going to say there is a hypothetical purchaser, you are saying what somebody would do if he existed, if the property was for sale, and a whole series of other very big "ifs." Actually, all he has to do is pay the amount of money so that when he is free, he has had the return on his money and the return of his money, in which case the sinking fund could be the proper rate. And you could wade out a little deeper and determine whether you should use a safe rate or the going rate on the recapture of your investment. My personal preference would be to capitalize prior to depreciation and use the Inwood concept, rather than the Hoskold concept.

The other idea in the straight-line concept is that it is a lot easier to do because if you use the sinking-fund concept, you have to determine what the average life of the property is, and unless you have a substantial staff that could work on engineering studies instead of the composite depreciation rate of this particular utility company, you have some real problems in determining the remaining life over which you must make the sinking-fund payments in order to recapture your investment.

It is much easier if you could live with the concept that the depreciation accruals will maintain the present property in its present state of repair. Then the straight-line is the easier and more pleasant way to go. But if you are going to say that you are going to use a definitive life, then you must have a staff that will come up with what is the average remaining economic life of the property.

Martin: Clyde, there is another question that is linked up with that. It may be linked up implicitly and not explicitly—that is, most of the federal agencies and maybe all of them require the application of straight-line depreciation to most properties of public service corporations, although I am not sure that this particular observation has any connection with Ron's methods in California. But it seems to me that it is worth raising the issue to allow us to think through whether or not it does have any merit in this application.

Fisher: Well, you are right back to book value versus market value. That is the distinction you always have to keep track of.

Martin: I think it all has to do with the rate at which the corporation recovers its investment and that is all that I was trying to point out. I am not sure that we have to consider one to the exclusion of the other.

Reeves: You are making the point that the claims on the income stream is where the real issue lies.

Martin: Yes, because the two methods of computed depreciation will have different effects within the period for which depreciation is computed—that is, they will affect different years differently. One will affect it one way, and one will affect it another way.

Fisher: If you capitalize prior to depreciation, then you will wipe out that regulatory attitude or the allowance that regulatory agencies make for recapture of investment, and then you make depreciation a function of value and that seems to me what we are trying to answer at this point.

Brasfield: Can you really divorce the whole thing from guideline depreciation? Wouldn't the prospective purchaser be tied to the same depreciation schedule as the existing owner?

Fisher: Now you are right back to what we were talking about before. From a market point of view, you do not care what the books are doing. The real questions are how much can you afford to pay for these properties, and how fast do you want to get your money back, and how much of a return do you want on your investment while it is tied up?

Martin: Doesn't the allowed depreciation by the regulatory body have some effect on the prospects of the value of having the property?

Fisher: Not if you do it prior to depreciation—you wash it out.

Welch: What if the regulatory authority uses straight-line depreciation? Wouldn't that mean that in their regulation of a utility's income stream, they assume a declining income over the life of the property in existence on the appraisal date—as contrasted with sinking-fund depreciation that assumes a level income stream?

McSwain: The Inwood or annuity method assumes a steady income stream.

Estimating Income

Reeves: Now I think we should turn our attention to the problem of determining what is the income that should be capitalized, and I would like to ask Ron Welch to lead off with this topic.

Welch: There has been a great deal written about income to be capitalized, and there is one of the chapters in the NATA report of 1954 that addresses itself entirely to determining the income to be capitalized. All the literature stresses the important thing that we are looking for is the future income and not the past income. Nearly everyone who wrestles with appraisal problems is aware of this fact. Past income does play a role in that it helps you estimate the future: It gives you a guide as to what the future may hold.

There are times, of course, when you just stop with the past income because by looking only to income from presently existing property, you do not see any substantial change looming up in the foreseeable future. If a growing income stream from a substantially unchanged plant has had a well-defined rate of growth in the past, then it is reasonable to assume that it will have that same kind of growth rate in the foreseeable future. In the case of a growing income stream resulting, apparently, from increasing investment, you would take a much shorter past period as your indicator of future income—that is, you go back a much shorter distance than if you had a stable income stream.

If you had a decreasing income stream, you would use the more recent period as being the best indicator of the future direction of the income. Looking at the past history, you may detect certain years that show abnormal incomes, and it may be that the abnormality is explainable. In the case of a hydroelectric plant, it could be that a year of very low rainfall might have resulted in low generating capacity and hence low income. I think these are the things you must consider when estimating future income.

Of course, there are some things in which there are differences in practice from place to place and state to state. Some state tax administrators will take a look at past income and use a five-year average, some a ten-year average; I think I recall one state a few years back that was using a fifteen-year average. I certainly would regard that kind of indicator of future income as being totally unacceptable because you are reaching much further into the past than I believe is proper.

However, I think the major questions in estimating future income revolve around depreciation and income tax. We in California, and I think for good reasons, capitalize before deducting both of these items. And I should point out when I am talking about income tax, I am talking about corporate income tax, not personal income tax.

The appraisal profession generally will capitalize income before deductions for depreciation. This technique is widely recognized and accepted by fee appraisers, and yet I find that in a good many states the tax administrators are taking the income after depreciation as the amount to be capitalized. Of course, you have to put a depreciation component into your capitalization rate if you are capitalizing before deducting depreciation as an expense or you must work with a terminating income instead of a perpetual income. You can take care of depreciation either way. I once saw a good appraiser do it both ways at once, which I think is rather cute. This appraiser came into the State Board of Equalization on behalf of a taxpayer and used a terminating income stream after he had already deducted depreciation as an expense item, and of course, that approach does not make any sense whatsoever because one is just a substitute for the other. But as to what kind of depreciation, I must confess that I am ambivalent on this. I am not certain about what kind of a depreciation factor you should put into a capitalization rate. A typical fee appraiser will put in a straight-line factor. If the property has a twenty-five-year economic life, he will add 4 percent to the interest rate.

Martin: You mean four percentage points, don't you?

Welch: Yes, that is what I mean. If it were 10 percent for the interest rate, then you would add 4 percent and have a capitalization rate of 14 percent. Of course, this straight-line method of recapture is the equivalent to having a declining income stream over the economic life of the property being appraised. There is a mathematical formula for estimating the decline rate of the income stream. I believe the formula is generally stated as $(I \times D)/(I + D) =$ the rate of decline, where I is interest rate and D is the recapture rate. The rate of decline will be the percent that income reduces each year.

I believe the Inwood premise (which I call the sinking-fund premise, while other people reserve the sinking-fund term for the Hoskold premise) assumes a constant income stream that terminates at some future date. The factors are chosen with the thought in mind that the income does not go on out into perpetuity. We add this factor to the rate that reflects the cost of capital. I believe this would produce a cap rate at the lower end of an acceptable range. Of course, what we are doing here is capitalizing cash flow, or discounting cash flow. It is not quite the cash flow that I was taught by Irving Fisher, but I think it will suffice to call it cash flow for our purposes.

One of the things that is done by very few appraisers is to capitalize income before deduction of federal corporate income taxes or federal and state corporate income taxes. This calls for injecting an income tax component into the capitalization rate. This idea was developed some twenty years ago, to the best of my knowledge, and I think first appeared in a publication by the American Society of Appraisers. One of the California people, Blair Hutson, of our Valuation Division, adapted the formula to the appraisal of utilities. Our formula is not quite right now because of changes in corporate income tax laws—graduated rates and changes in depreciation allowances—but it probably comes within the tolerance that must be accorded in many aspects of utility valuation. The formula is: Income Tax Rate $\times$ (Basic Rate of Return $+$ Depreciation Component of the Cap Rate $-$ 1/Economic Life $-$ Borrowed Capital Component of the Cap Rate)/(1 $-$ Income Tax Rate). (Of course, one could reason all of these things out and would not have to use this particular mathematical formula.) Incidentally, I am using the "Basic Rate of Return" here to indicate the rate of return computed by the band-of-investment method that we talked about earlier in this conversation.

I forgot to mention earlier that you do not deduct property taxes from the income stream, but you include a component for property taxes in the cap rate at the actual effective rate—the percent of market value that is paid in property tax each year. Of course, this concept is important for property tax appraisers because to do anything other than include the property tax component in the cap rate would be to indicate you already knew the value of the property when you started out your calculations and therefore knew what the property tax would actually be. I think this is a great deal more important for property tax appraisers than for fee appraisers in the regular course of their work.

So the total capitalization rate is the sum of the basic rate of return, the depreciation component, the income tax component, and the property tax component. In an appraisal I made recently of a rather loosely regulated enterprise, a cable television system, the figures I assigned to these parts of the cap rate were 14.3 percent, 3.23 percent, 3.81 percent, and 3.12 percent, respectively.

There are a lot of other little refinements that I suppose should be mentioned and of course you will find these mentioned in the other reports. The Western States Report of 1971 shows it like this:

$$t = \frac{I(A - \frac{1}{L} - B_i)}{1.00 - I},$$

where t = Tax per dollar of capitalized value;

I = Income tax rate (federal plus state, for intrastate companies; federal only for interstate companies);

A = Rate of return plus sinking-fund annuity at that same rate;

L = Life expectancy;

B = Percentage of long-term debt in capital structure;

i = Interest rate on long-term debt.

Reeves: Dr. Martin, would you like to pursue this particular area of discussion?

Martin: I would think that one of the important things by way of future looks at this would be to test that basic rate. I should say the *aggregate* rate, not the *basic* rate in your sense of the word, and what I mean by testing it is to find some way of measuring that rate against what actually occurs in the market to determine whether this is the rate that applies in the actual sales transactions that we are able to verify in the informed marketplace.

I should point out that the figures that Ron has just stated look all right to me, so I am not suggesting there is anything wrong with them. I am just saying they could be verified or tested if we could find actual sales for which we had the income information. By making that kind of comparison, we would know whether these are rates that could be used safely to estimate value of other properties for which we know only the income.

If we could make these kinds of tests and find that they are right, we would be making a real contribution toward the universal acceptability of this type of calculation. If we could develop some overall acceptable test, as we have been working toward in Kentucky, I think we would be doing a great deal for the appraisal profession.

Unfortunately, we do not have the stock-and-debt method of valuation available to us anymore to the extent we once did since so many companies are conglomerate in their operation, and it is very difficult to identify the actual portion of the company's structure that is used in the actual utility operation. There are some areas, of course, where we do have fairly good information, certainly electric power plants and telephone companies, where the operating utility is the sole or major part of the company's business. I find that we do get good stock-and-debt information for this type of property.

Now the figures that Ron has put on the board might be a little high for standard utility companies, such as I just mentioned. However, for the cable television industry, those may be just exactly the right figures to be using because there is difference in the structure and risk of those companies.

Welch: Yes, I think the basic interest rate would be lower for the well-established, regulated utility properties in which the service is regarded as a necessity as compared to cable television in which the service might be more of a luxury item. Also, the life expectancy of cable television equipment is substantially less than that of public utility equipment, so there would be a difference in the rate included for depreciation or recovery of interest.

Reeves: Dr. Martin, do you have any other suggestions that might relate specifically to methodology?

Martin: I hope to have, as we go deeper into the stock-and-debt method as a way of getting a better estimate of the true value of a reasonably representative bunch of corporations. They will not necessarily be the corporations that we are valuing except now and then. They will be corporations that could be any place in the United States, and the important thing will be the availability of the basic information that we need. Remember, we are talking about market value, and since the market for larger types of public utility companies is a national market, we do not really have to worry about from whose experience we are getting the market data. We do not have to worry about applying this to California or corporations in another state simply because the same market would be available to investors in either case.

In this way, we would be testing the market behavior, and we would want to test it in exactly the manner in which Ron has put this down. I think anything that can help refine our work would be a major contribution, and I can see already from looking at this particular piece of work that it represents a substantial improvement over the capitalization of just net railway operating income or net operating income for another type of utility property.

Reeves: Professor Bonbright, do you have any comments you would like to make at this point?

Bonbright: No, but I must say I am very much impressed. The procedure outlined by Ron Welch looks very, very good to me.

Woolery: I would like to ask Ron whether he would just run through the steps and show us how he comes down to the income to be capitalized—that is, starting with the gross income and then getting us down to the actual income that is capitalized into an estimate of value.

Welch: First, you deduct all expenses except interest, property tax, depreciation, and income tax. I do not think we need to get into an argument about what are deductible expenses; that is outside of this discussion. Excise taxes would not be left in, they would be deducted as a cost of doing business.

McSwain: Well, I have several questions that might bring out some points here. One thing, Ron, you use an average of income. Would you average over a three-year period?

Welch: No, we almost always use one year on a growing utility—especially those that are very stable anyway, such as the telephone and power companies. We used a multi-year average for the railroads, which in spite of their stability as a business, do have year-to-year fluctuations that can be quite large.

McSwain: You say you use one year, but if you were to use three years on a rapidly growing utility, say, one that was growing at 10 percent or 15 percent or even 20 percent a year, would you adjust the income for the past two or three years for the increase in plant, because the income three years ago would be entirely different from the income today in that the income three years ago represented the plant three years ago and there have been substantial additions since then?

Welch: Yes, that would be all right.

McSwain: And my next point is, suppose this were an electric utility that had $200 million work in progress and the regulatory commission does not permit that utility to earn on the work in progress, would you actually adjust—that is add some income to represent the work in progress—because the potential purchaser of this company would anticipate a future income stream when the work in progress went into the rate base?

Welch: Yes, I think we would do that. However, you do run into some problems, and I am not sure I know the answers to them. Some of the work in progress is just replacing some existing plant, so you are just trading some old plant for some new plant, and with this thought in mind in California we used a fraction of the total work in progress as part of the total taxable value.

Reeves: What would be wrong with adding to the value estimate produced by capitalizing earnings the actual cost of the work in progress? That is the alternative I would find acceptable.

McSwain: Well, another problem that we bump into is that some of these nuclear plants will not go on-line and begin producing electricity for six, seven, and even eight years. So, the construction work in progress will not actually be earning for that period in time, and it would be my inclination to discount that income back to a present worth. So, the portion of construction work in progress that would not begin earning until some future date should have its imputed earnings discounted to a present worth.

Welch: You would not discount the cost of it?

McSwain: No. You discount the projected income stream for the date it will begin earning to the present time.

Welch: I definitely would not discount the cost.

McSwain: That is right, we discount the future income that the construction work in progress will earn. There is another point I would like to discuss here, and that is in reference to your use of the straight-line and Inwood. Now unless you gyrate your figures, if you use the same recapture period—that is, depreciation period—if you use straight-line, which assumes a declining income stream, or use the annuity method, which presumes a level income stream, then your valuations by the annuity technique would be much higher than the other valuation. So, unless you do some adjusting with your figures, you are going to come out with a much higher value estimate if you use the Inwood factor instead of straight-line. We are appraising the property as of a given date, and that property is going to have a declining income stream because it is getting older and wearing out, and next year when we appraise the property again, we are appraising a different property. Some, of course, will be the same property, a little older, but there will be some new property that has been added to it, so that does not mean that next year you have to look at something lower because there will be the addition of new property.

Martin: May I raise another kind of question here? Let's look at the income tax component and view it in light of the present situation with the present income tax deferrals. What do you do with the current year's deferrals, and what do you do with the amounts that were deferred in previous years? Remember, that what has already been deferred is sometimes a whale of a figure.

Welch: Well, right or wrong, we don't do anything with what has already been deferred; that is water over the dam. We are looking to the future, and as I said, I don't know whether we are right about this, but we have not allowed for any difference between the deferred income tax and the income tax that is not deferred. We are capitalizing income before income tax, and that means income before income tax whether it is paid in the year in which it is due or deferred until some future date. Then we have computed the income tax component of the capitalization rate by the method I outlined earlier. I must say I don't know what it does in the area of deferrals.

Fisher: It is the equivalent of normalizing the federal income tax, and you may be avoiding the argument about whether the deferred taxes are worth anything to the person who has them and whether they should be valued as part of the property. So what you are assuming is that they are going to pay taxes at the 48 percent normalized rate, while in fact maybe in the early life of the property they do not pay all of their liability, but later on, as the property gets older, they will be paying at a higher rate, and it will all even out over the life of the property.

Coffey: What about treatment of the investment credit?

Welch: I think that is part of the same picture.

Fisher: That is another thing in that you have an outright tax credit at the very start.

Coffey: Well, you never pay that.

Fisher: You aren't expected to because that is just an outright tax credit. It is really a government gift that you are allowed to deduct at the end of your return, but that is a different problem from the deferred federal income tax.

Oldman: But in your income stream, do you include that investment tax credit as part of the income to be capitalized?

Fisher: We have on the assumption that the law is always going to be there and that the additions are going to be at the same rate that they were in the current year.

McSwain: I think what Mr. Fisher is doing is simply ignoring any special benefits to the taxpayer from the federal income tax legislation and is interpreting the basic income tax law without any special provisions and saying over the long haul that everything is going to average out. If someone builds a $1 billion nuclear plant, we cannot assume that there is going to be a billion dollar plant every year. But if you wash out those big surges in the investment tax credit, you can reasonably assume that there is going to be an investment tax credit unless you can demonstrate something completely contrary, and you have seen as well as I have the great variations. It has varied from three to seven to eleven and back down again, depending upon the state of the national economy. Maybe we are unfair in applying today's rate; maybe we ought to take the average of the last five years.

Recapturing Capital

Reeves: I am not completely clear here. In one instance, you come in before income taxes and that eliminates the problem of future income tax deferrals, and you come in before depreciation and that eliminates the problem of income tax credits. And by adopting the method that Ron Welch just outlined, you do not get involved with the tax structure and depreciation however it might be calculated.

Martin: I guess that would be true if the figure that we looked at is right.

Fisher: You eliminate the regulatory effect on depreciation. Whatever they allow, you say we will just wash that out and the appraiser will use his judgment, so you effectively wash out the regulatory attitude toward depreciation.

Reeves: In effect what Ron would do here is provide for the recouping of capital through the capitalization rate without reference to depreciation in the income stream.

Welch: Right.

McSwain: Yes, but it depends upon the adjustments you make to the income stream. If you adjust the income stream, then you have to adjust the cap rate. Of course, if your adjustments are right, you are going to come up with the same answers no matter whether you adjust the income stream or the cap rate.

74

Welch: I think Don Fisher just raised a point on which I equivocated earlier. I said I did not know whether we should use the straight-line depreciation component or the sinking-fund factor, and I guess I was really talking about the Inwood factor. If the regulatory commission uses straight-line depreciation—and I think they all do—and regulates your income effectively on that kind of a basis, then I think that is what you ought to use in your capitalization-of-earnings approach, because the property that you hold on the assessment date is going to be allowed to earn a return including straight-line depreciation and not including depreciation by some other method. This raises a question in my mind about the approach we are using.

McSwain: I think probably you have been using straight-line, Hoskold, and Inwood interchangeably, and really these are three different things.

Welch: Yes, I agree with you, Bob, and we should point out that sinking-fund recapture implies that you are making annual periodic deposits with accumulating compound interest, and at the end of the life of the property, the sinking-fund will equal the price you paid for the property going in.

Reeves: I always thought that the Hoskold formula had two different rates, a risk rate and a safe rate, and that the risk rate applied to the return you were earning on your investment and the safe rate applied to the interest on the sinking-fund portion that is set aside to recapture the original investment.

Welch: That is right. The Hoskold premise is typically a capitalization method in which the two rates differ. The Inwood premise is a special case of the Hoskold in which the risk rate and safe rate are the same.

Woolery: That would be the same as the Ellwood if there were no mortgage because then you would be calculating the sinking-fund factor at the risk rate, and the overall rate would simply be the yield rate on equity plus the sinking fund factor at the equity yield rate.

Welch: I agree with you. I think there is some literature to support the viewpoint that Ellwood and Inwood really produce identical results, but Inwood is shown as a factor and Ellwood is shown as a rate, so one would simply be the reciprocal of the other.

Woolery: Yes. But I think it might be wiser to confine sinking-fund recovery to wasting assets such as mining properties where ore bodies have a definite period of life, and that way you would simply accumulate in the sinking fund enough to liquidate your original investment over the life of the mining property. However, when you are talking about utility properties, at least in theory, the utility or public service corporation is going to go on indefinitely adding new property all the time, and that might be a good reason for employing straight-line recapture. However, we may be confusing the business itself with the utility plant that is actually used in the business. The utility plant has a finite life, and it is the value of the utility plant that we are trying to recapture over the useful life or economic life of the asset. So maybe it does not make much difference what you employ as a method of recapturing the original asset investment as long as you conform to what is being used by real investors in the real world.

Fisher: I think we are theorizing again to a certain extent, and what we should really do is look to see what the market is doing and what the typical investor in the marketplace is doing and be guided by his actions. I observe that very few if any investors are setting aside periodic sinking-fund payments at some particular safe rate of return as a way of recouping their investment at the end of the useful life of the assets.

Construction Work in Progress

Bonbright: I think I would like to come back to the handling of construction work in progress and how that is valued. Recently I have read that one or more regulatory commissions will allow construction work in progress to go right into the rate base.

Welch: I think it only goes into the rate base when it goes on stream and becomes part of the operating property of the utility plant.

Reeves: Ron, times are changing. I had occasion to look into this particular matter last summer. The utility companies, of course, are pushing to get construction work in progress into the rate base right away and, I might add, they are meeting with considerable success, I think, especially with the Federal Power Commission. I know the Federal Power Commission is considering letting the construction work in progress into the rate base, at least under certain conditions, and there are certain states that have the same type of consideration in mind. If they do not let it in, it seems to me that construction work in progress is going to keep building up, and it might be better if the rate bases were augmented by something like 5 percent per annum in order to make some allowance for this construction work in progress.

There is a very real basis for handling construction work in progress differently for rate-making purposes, than for property tax valuation purposes. I can make a very good argument for putting it into the rate-making process because the money is actually invested. As matters now stand, you do not start getting your money back until the construction work is finished, so the construction work in progress is not income producing until it goes into the operating plant. So there is a very good argument for not getting it into the income stream for property tax purposes, but having it as an add-on on a cost basis until it becomes productive.

Welch: I don't care which way you handle it. You can either handle it as an add-on at its stated cost, or you can impute some future earnings to it and capitalize those future earnings into an indication of value. Of course, you should come out with the same result because the dollar amount of construction work in progress should constitute the present worth of the future income that the construction work will earn, or else somebody has made a bad investment.

It seems to me what you should do is put in the construction work in progress as a nonearning asset at just exactly what it costs so it would be subject to ad valorem tax on the basis of the property that is there. You would include the interest charges during construction as one of the costs that would go into the final rate base as well as the tax base.

Coffey: What about the handling of something like a substantial deposit on equipment for future delivery? That is for a major generator or generating plant you might make an advance deposit of $25 million, but there still is no physical equipment to show for that deposit. So it seems to me you must get an analysis of the construction account, and then you would have to identify those portions of the account that represent nothing more than deposits or down payments for equipment that will be delivered sometime in the future.

Welch: I think another aspect is that that particular property might not be within your jurisdiction. It might be a California utility making a down payment on a generator that would be fabricated in Pennsylvania or New York, and it actually would not be in the state in which the utility valuation is being made for tax purposes. Of course, it may be taxed in South Philadelphia where the fabrication is actually taking place and where it is part of the inventory of manufactured goods, but it certainly would not be taxable to a California utility company at that time.

McCreath: How about such things as architectural fees and engineering design fees that are paid in advance of actual construction? How would they be excluded from the construction work in progress?

Welch: Our theory has always been that those particular fees are absorbed over the entire construction phase. You do not really tax them in advance even though the services may have been rendered in advance; you spread them over the life of the construction phase of the project. I must say, I don't know what kind of practical problems we find in carrying out this policy, but at least that is what we are trying to do.

Morrison: Do you expense that item, or do you capitalize it?

Reeves: You capitalize it.

Welch: Yes, that is right, you capitalize it. But you do not capitalize it until you start constructing the tangible property. At least for tax purposes you do not do that.

Coffey: But it would be sitting in the deferred credit account, then, wouldn't it?

Welch: I think so.

Coffey: If you stop and think about it, in the case of that nuclear plant that Bob was talking about earlier going in with an eventual investment of $4 billion, you will accumulate tremendous costs in the construction account before they move that first shovel full of dirt. We might need to get back to a better definition of real property.

Welch: There is no question there are some hazards here, and it is possible that something could get assessed completely improperly.

Reeves: Well, as soon as you have one steel post in the ground, I suppose all of those costs could be attached to it.

Fisher: Ron, we are trying something in Oregon now, and we don't know whether it will succeed or not. Portland General Electric Company is building a $1 billion nuclear plant and plans to build a second $1 billion plant at the same location. They have about $1 million in land, and I would guess they have another million for a hole in the ground. Last year, we put about $14 million on engineering drawings and plans and payments they have made to Bechtel Corporation down in San Francisco, and this year those charges are going to be up around $55 million. And we put this on the roll as being taxable in Oregon as intangible property. It is not tangible property yet, but under our law we can assess intangibles. They have started construction, there is land and some construction; so we have said O.K., this has a situs in Oregon. We do not know if we will survive in the courts, but we will try anyway.[d]

Reeves: If you have a law on the books that permits you to tax intangibles, I would think you have a pretty good case.

Fisher: We have such a law.

---

[d]See Appendix C.

Reeves: I raise the question, suppose you had only a hole in the ground, then has it become tangible? If that hole were made in keeping with the design for the final plant, then the value would be $55 million, and that hole would be a valuable piece of real estate.

Fisher: Write for our free booklet, and we will tell you.

Franzman: Clyde, as a matter of adding more complications or discussions on the construction work in progress, there is another problem in addition to the exclusion of things because they are not on site yet and therefore may be viewed as intangibles for the present. We also have the problem of trying to distinguish between property that is carried as construction work in progress but is actually intended to replace plant already in existence and operation. Therefore, it is already included in the current valuation by the cost approach, and its income is already included in the capitalization of earnings estimate. So, we temper our estimate of the value of construction work in process accordingly.

Reeves: I think Ron would certainly concur on this, and I believe he has already made that point.

Welch: Yes, if you use a short period for the income you are capitalizing. However, you don't have a lot of that, but even during the one-year time that we use, there is likely to be some of it.

Martin: How do you get the data for that?

Welch: Do I have to tell you?

Franzman: We trust our taxpayers to report their estimates for these figures.

Fisher: If you had built a new transmission line or if you had added a new generating facility, these things could be sorted out. Then the balance would be the run-of-the-mill construction work in progress just to replace or maintain the present property.

Fleming: Seth, are you assuming there is going to be something in the construction work in progress to replace some of the existing plant—that is, something will be taken out of the present plant and something new inserted in its place—so that in effect some of this present construction work in progress is really replacement plant?

Franzman: Let me illustrate. If an existing transmission line had to be moved because a highway was being widened, the cost of relocating that line would be carried under construction work in progress, but its function and earning capacity would be the same after it was moved as before the move was made. Then we would view that line or plant as performing the same function and generating the same income to be capitalized after the move as it did before the move. So, therefore, that particular plant would have no effect on the total value even though there had been substantial construction work in progress associated with it. However, if the plant were upgraded at the same time to increase its earning capacity and therefore its value, we would certainly make an adjustment in the final value estimates.

McSwain: We have the same situation with a small telephone company that borrowed a lot of REA money and built a complete new telephone system. The old system stood there in use while the new system was under construction. When the new one was completed, they just shut down the old one and salvaged whatever copper wire and other materials that was possible. I think that would be the same type of situation where you have replaced existing plant but have also upgraded it, so you have two considerations—that is, the consideration of just the replacement of the existing plant and of course the extra value generated from the upgrading.

Martin: I am interested in exploring the problem of say AT&T, which in its new conduits or new cables is able to send thousands and thousands of messages over one cable. Most of that is replacing property that was in use previously.

Franzman: Yes, but there is generally the addition of new capacity, so you have the upgrading also.

Martin: That is the point that I don't think we have mentioned yet. What you are saying about the additional capacity is that it would be new plant and it would represent added value to the unit.

Capitalization Rates for Cable Television

Reeves: I think that Bruce Taylor has something to add.

Taylor: I am interesting in the approach to calculating the capitalization rate that was set out by Ron Welch earlier in the conversation. This is the first time I have ever seen this approach, and I was wondering whether they use that 52.58 percent for the income tax component calculation all the way through the entire formula before they came up with the final cap rate. I'm asking: Is it being put in twice or has it already been excluded by adding the income tax back to the income to be capitalized and then compensated for in the capitalization rate?

Welch: I think you are being put off a little bit by the basic rate of 14.3 percent. This is applied to a cable television system, and I used a post–income tax return on equity of 16 percent. The company was able to borrow money at an effective rate of something over 13 percent. By the band-of-investment method, we came up with 14.5 percent as the cost of capital. I think we had a debt/equity mix of 55/45, so there would be a weight of 55 on the 11 percent money and a weight of 45 percent on the 16 percent equity return, and that is how we came back to the weighted average of 14.3 percent. There is no income tax element in the basic rate.

Coffey: Ron, that last statement you made disturbs me a little bit. You said their equity rate was 16 percent and their debt was at 11 percent.

Welch: It was more than 11 percent, but I can't remember the exact figure.

Coffey: Were you looking at their books on both instances there?

Welch: No. The actual figure for debt, I find by consulting my notes, was 11.25 percent and the 16 percent was based upon what I thought equity investors in cable television systems are actually looking for as a rate of return. I did examine what the stock market was saying about Viacom and other cable television issues. I think as of the appraisal date for the particular cable company in question, we are looking at typical yields in the cable television equity area of 15 percent to 16 percent. So we actually got that equity yield rate from the market.

McSwain: Was the interest rate they were paying and the market rate the same?

Welch: I am not sure, but I think they were.

McSwain: I was wondering why you used the actual rate they were paying rather than the market rate?

Welch: I think they were both about the same. I think, Bob, they were paying 1 percent over prime with a 25 percent compensating balance. At the time in question, the cost of borrowed capital came out to about 11.25 percent. I would have to assume that any buyer of the company would be putting the company's assets up for security and would have to pay the same kind of interest rate to get the money.

Reeves: I guess this would be a good time to break things off for today. In tomorrow's conversations we should put a little more emphasis on research methods of testing the validity of the capitalization rate hypotheses that we may have been making during today's conversation. I have a feeling that this is a critical item as sustaining input for any of us who wish to use the methods. Tomorrow we also should discuss the difference between a valuation and an assessment or an appraisal and an assessment. When are you justified in departing from a valuation by averaging or otherwise to get an assessment that does not do violence to either the taxpayer or the taxing jurisdiction—the leveling of the tax load, in other words?

And so ended the first day of conversations about valuation.

Second Day

Valuing Companies that Do Not Have Publicly Traded Securities

McSwain: I have been thinking about some of the things we talked about yesterday, and I do have a question, especially for Dr. Martin. Possibly Ron Welch will wish to comment on this question also. Dr. Martin seems to like the stock-and-debt approach to valuation of public service corporations and he commented yesterday that it is becoming more and more difficult to use the stock-and-debt approach because you have so many companies in which stock is not being traded—that is, it is being closely held. I would like to have Dr. Martin's comment on an approach I have used for valuing a corporation whose stock is closely held and not apt to be traded, so there is no established market price for it.

Let's say, for instance, we have a telephone company whose stock and maybe debt also is held by AT&T and none of it is being publicly traded. If I were to go to Standard & Poor's, I could find maybe thirty or thirty-five different telephone companies listed. I could find other types of companies also. These companies would have stock that is actively traded, and we might find that the stock is selling for eleven times earnings. After careful analysis, I come to the conclusion that typically the stock in this particular sample of companies is selling for eleven times earnings. Let's also say the sample includes thirty to thirty-five telephone companies that actually show a price-earnings ratio of eleven. Then I would like to ask Dr. Martin if he were to take the net income of the subject property whose stock is not publicly traded and multiply that net income by eleven, the price-earnings ratio, to get an indication of the expected price per share of stock, would that be an acceptable method of valuing the equity of the subject company?

Martin: No, I think you have to do some other things too, Bob. It is my feeling that there is a wide range of cross-checks that you can make. I do not think that I would put my primary reliance on the price-earnings ratio as a value indicator.

Given my choice, I would put the operating ratio ahead of the price-earnings ratio as a value indicator. The operating ratio tells you a lot about the basic prosperity of a company, and it will give you a really good indication of where problems may lie with the company. It will tell you whether you have trouble in your measuring stick for what you are measuring. I am not really wedded to the operating ratio, but I think it is more reliable by far than the price-earnings ratio.

I should say I also like the concept of using your price-earnings ratio as a way of translating earnings into expected selling prices for shares of stock. I certainly would want to use that along with the other indices that would indicate the basic financial health of the company. Also, I would want to look at the operating ratio and take an average of perhaps three or four years just to see what is the typical figure for the company or sample of companies in question.

Choose the best telephone capitalization rates for three or four different levels of income and you can make value estimates superior to those you can compute by the method you describe. Still it is useful as a check.

McSwain: I appreciate that answer, but in some cases in a sample, twenty or more would show a price-earnings ratio of eleven and most of the rest would run ten or twelve. Then you might have three or four showing price-earnings ratios as high as eighteen or twenty or as low as three or four. So after you have thoroughly examined the figures for the subject property and its various ratios, would you feel safe in using eleven as your price-earnings multiple for the subject property if the rest of its characteristics were similar to companies in the sample having price-earnings ratios of eleven?

Martin: Yes, if I had checked it as thoroughly as you have indicated, I certainly would use eleven. I think the point you are raising is similar to the one Ron raised yesterday with his cable television appraisal. There, if you recall, he was taking Viacom as his indicator, and I think you are always better off to have a large sample of companies. I think you are on sound ground when you base your market indication on a relatively large sample of similar companies.

McSwain: Now along the same line in developing the stock-and-debt approach to value, let's suppose that you have bonds in the company that are not trading actively in the public market. I normally go to the comprehensive bond guide where you can determine the current rate, that is the indicated yield to maturity, and from that I get the estimated current market value of the debt.

Martin: That is fine, if we can find quotations for other bonds of the same corporation or for a corporation with similar characteristics. I think this is especially true of senior bonds, but I think it becomes more tricky in the case of equipment obligations. I think there are some other financial publications somewhat more obscure than Moody's and Standard & Poor's that give that information about the selling prices of debt instruments and equipment trust certificates, and you can, if you are persistent enough, dig out some information of this type that is very helpful in valuing this kind of property. We find that the particular publication that I have in mind does quote occasional sales, and it certainly seems to me that one occasional sale might have more value than twenty estimates for doing a rigorous appraisal. While I make estimates just as all of us have to do, I feel a lot more comfortable when I can back up those estimates with some verified sales data.

We did run some tests over about a two-year period, and we were able to find some AT&T affiliates, which did have some stock outstanding. There were not very many companies, and the amount of stock traded was very small, often as little as 2 percent and in no cases more than 8 percent of the total shares outstanding. But our evidence for the AT&T companies shows almost identical figures when compared with independent companies of the same general class— that is, when we tested them in the manner in which you suggested in your proposal.

I think that is important because there is a good deal of literature to the effect that if the whole issue is not on the market, then the quotations may be suspect. In this particular case, the evidence was to the contrary. I think the logic is to the contrary myself, but I might ask Ron Welch what he thinks about that.

Welch: I agree with you, Jim, that the logic is to the contrary in this particular case. I think this is important because there are frequent references in literature by competent scholars that the results won't stand up if you only have a small fraction of the securities traded on the open market. But apparently, based on the studies we have made so far, that is just not so. You have to recognize that the tests that have been made so far have been limited to one kind of company and just one particular class of stock.

Brasfield: Dr. Martin, as I understood what you were saying, you were speaking about bonds outstanding. Did you mean that a small amount of bonds was outstanding or a small amount of stock was outstanding?

Martin: Both. Actually, the procedure is the same for stock or for bonds. Of course, bonds are harder to test, and the tests are less adequate. Most of the independents are not rated AAA, and most of the AT&T companies are rated AAA. Of course, I'm talking about the senior bonds, which does make a difference, but in this particular case we use the ratings as a standard for comparison. In studying the stock, we used all the companies and that may be suspect, but I surely don't know. I like to get as broad a sample as possible before putting reliance on any kind of an indicator of this type. But I would advance the hypothesis that the stock and the bonds are both good indicators of value when you can get market data on them. We have found that there is a fairly substantial amount of stock on the open market for most of the companies we analyze.

Investment Tax Credit

Reeves: I think that Chuck McCreath has a question.

McCreath: Yes, I do have a question, but first I would like to make an explanation. I don't know whether we have the same manuals and publications that Dr. Martin is working with, but we did find that last year National Bank and Quotation Record came out for the first time with listings of trust certificates for railroads and the actual quotations of selling prices or market value. I believe this is the first year that has been done. We found the publication to be very comprehensive and very helpful for our purposes. And now to my question, I would like to ask Dr. Martin, Dr. Bonbright, and Dr. Welch for their comments on the first portion of it, and then I would like to address the second portion of it to the other people who are working in day-to-day property tax administration. I would like to ask them whether there is a practical application in what I am asking. My first question, though, to the panel is this: How do you feel that the investment tax credit should be handled in the income stream? Should it be handled as a deduction from income, or should it be flowed through and counted as net income in the year in which it is taken? That is the question I would like to ask the panel. Now, the question I would like to ask the tax administrators is: How many are excluding the investment tax credit and how many are letting it go through as an expense?

Reeves: Which question do you want to ask first?

McCreath: I would like to ask the panel first.

Martin: I don't know. I am still working on it.

Fisher: Probably, Chuck, what you should do is restate the question and explain the investment tax credit a little bit because some of the panel might be thinking in terms of deferred federal income tax. Maybe if you explain the history of investment tax credit, it might be helpful.

McCreath: During the Second World War, investment tax credit came in as an incentive for investment and it was looked upon more or less as a gift to a company that invested in certain classes of property. As I recall, it was about three percent at that time, and I hope Don will correct me if I am mistaken. Then, it was dropped for a few years, still leaving these figures on the books until a portion of the plant that was subject to the investment tax credit was removed. Then a few years ago, the federal government came out and brought the investment tax credit back in at the rate of 10 percent, and I believe there was a period of time during which they could bring some equipment into the plant and be allowed a 7 percent investment tax credit. I think there was a possibility of bringing the amount of the investment tax credit to 11 percent if 1 percent were dedicated to employee benefit plans, for example, Employee Stock Option Plan. So at the present time we have the possibility of 11 percent investment tax credit applicable to property that is purchased to go into the plant in certain categories. This is allowable as an expense in their income stream. For those of us who work in the utility valuation field, it is allowable as an above the line item in the expense account.

Fisher: Maybe we should wait just a minute and clear that up. You don't really call it an expense. The tax credit or investment tax credit is taken at the end of the income tax return, and what it actually does is decrease the amount of federal income tax that the company would otherwise be paying so that effectively it increases the income of the company.

Reeves: Am I to understand that you could defer 11 percent of the income tax by making the investments?

Fisher: No, no, no. That is not right. You would be allowed to take a credit of 11 percent of your purchases against the total income tax due. If you had purchased $1,000 of equipment, then you could take 11 percent of that or $110 off the actual income tax due at the very end of your income tax return. So, you would have your income tax reduced by an amount equal to 11 percent of the equipment purchased.

McCreath: The argument, of course, goes both ways. The utilities view this investment tax credit as being eventually plowed back as an income tax expense, and none of it really flows back into the income stream. We have other accountants who say that a portion of that will be allocated to income tax expense and the excess will eventually find its way into the income stream. So their argument is if we are to receive any of that as a legitimate income, it would be forthcoming some time in the future.

Reeves: Ron Welch, do you want to tackle that question?

Welch: I don't want to, but I am prepared to more out of ignorance than wisdom. As I understand it, this really amounts to a reduction in the cost of the property that you are purchasing. If you are making enough money to pay income tax, then this investment tax credit amounts to an 11 percent reduction in the price that you are paying for the equipment you are purchasing.

Coffey: We may have left out one item. Let's go back in the early 1960s when you got the 7 percent investment tax credit and in the case of utilities, 3 percent. You actually had to show the cost of equipment at the reduced figure on your depreciation schedule.

Welch: Don't you now?

Coffey: No. Now you get to depreciate the nominal purchase price of the property and not the purchase price minus the investment tax credit amount. So your property goes on the books at 100 percent of the stated purchase price.

Welch: Then doesn't the investment tax credit really amount to an outright gift from the federal government? Isn't that what it really amounts to? It appears to me that the federal government is paying for part of the property that the utility company is buying. I would say, and I must caution you this is purely theoretical. Since you are assessing property that exists on the lien date, this item really has nothing to do with the future income you should be capitalizing. You might call this income if you like, but it really has nothing to do with future income.

Fisher: Do you think it has anything to do with past income?

Welch: I am not really concerned with whether it has anything to do with past income, and I don't think it has anything to do with future income from the property that is in existence as of the lien date.

Fisher: Would you put it in utility operating income or would you exclude it?

Welch: I would exclude it.

Reeves: If we use, as has been suggested here, income before taxes, then this particular problem does not arise. Many states—and I assume from Chuck McCreath's remarks that Idaho is one—have a practice of using something approaching net operating income, and that is the reason we have the problem. So the question is what ought we to do under the circumstances in which we find ourselves in relation to this particular thing?

Welch: Let me qualify my statement further: Your treatment of the investment tax credit may well depend upon what the regulatory agency does with it.

Reeves: I don't think the regulatory agencies are concerned with the income stream.

Coffey: They are normalizing now.

Welch: You mean this has no bearing on the rate-making process?

Reeves: I don't think so because the utilities have persuaded the Federal Power Commission to issue a regulation to cover this item to their satisfaction.

Martin: Let me inject something here that may raise another question or reservation about this whole matter. This whole question is based upon law. It is a permanent law as far as the formula is concerned. It is on the books now, and as far as we know, it will continue to be the law. Now in that sense it forecasts the future. Does that impose upon you another reservation?

Welch: No, I don't think so because we are appraising the property that is actually in existence on the assessment date, and we are not appraising the property that is going to be purchased in the future.

Reeves: Arlo wants to either clarify or add to our existing confusion.

Woolery: I would really like to extend the question a little bit. If we are really finding market value, then our true concern is with what the buyer is going to pay to the present owner for this property. Is the buyer going to be concerned with the fact that there was an investment tax credit to the seller at one time? So, in finding the market value of the company, is the whole question of the investment tax credit germane to the valuation issue? I think that gets you to Ron's point of view that he is not concerned with the seller; he is concerned only with the buyer in the appraisal process, and that may lead to the second part of my question or statement, whichever it turns out to be. Dr. Martin stated earlier in the conversation that we are going to be forced to rely more and more on the capitalized earnings indicator for valuation in the absence of sound market data, especially in the case of conglomerate ownership of utility and railroad property. Also, Dr. Martin says we have just about foreclosed using cost data. So if we are to fall back on the single indicator of capitalized earnings, do we have to concern ourselves with the investment tax credit at all? We may be muddying up some clear water in trying to handle Chuck McCreath's question.

Reeves: I am going to exercise the prerogative of the Chair for a moment. It is my observation that utilities are going to insist that the investment tax credit does not properly belong in the income stream. They will say they are putting it into a special trust fund—so what is wrong with taking it out of the income stream and adding it on down at the bottom? Doesn't that trust fund add to the value of the company?

Coffey: What is wrong with normalizing the deferred credit and reducing the federal income tax for the life of the property, which is now standard accounting procedure? To my knowledge, it is acceptable for nearly everybody with the possible exception of a few western states. The 1971 Western States study recommended using investment tax credits as an addition to income, or a reduction of federal income taxes paid in the one year the reduction was allowed as an offset to the tax liability, therefore, increasing the income to be capitalized. So they in effect were following the flow-through concept for the investment tax credit, as I am told was originally required by many state regulatory bodies as well as was practiced by many utility companies, notably, the American Electric Power Company.

Reeves: The American Electric Power Company did originally, but it has changed now.

Coffey: To my knowledge, all parties have now changed and are rejecting flow-through accounting for the investment tax credit, which certainly does not amount to an additional income of $20 million, unless there is a tax liability that was created due to the activities throughout the rest of the company. Assuming there is a tax liability, would not an income statement reflecting a gradual cut-in of this tax credit be far superior for our purpose rather than one that produces a 20 percent or 30 percent increase in income in those years where a power plant was put in service?

Reeves: I would like to recognize Gerald McDougall, and then I will get back to Coleman.

McDougall: I just wanted to put additional stress on the point that Don Fisher was making earlier, and then push things back in Ron Welch's direction. I feel this is really an important question. You have to be concerned about its effect on historic income because it definitely has to enter in somewhere in the time frame. In effect, it is not just historic income and of no more concern. Ron says it does not affect future income. I think it does enter in the first period of the future following that period in which it was taken. In my opinion, this is where it affects the income stream. If an investor were purchasing the company before the end of the tax year, he would certainly receive the advantage of the investment tax credit, and this will affect his investment decision—that is, how much he is willing to pay for that company.

Coffey: It also affects the seller, since he has to have recapture.

McCreath: I agree with the historical income portion with the exception that in our particular area, the Pacific Northwest, our growth rates are tremendous and our utility companies are actually doubling their plant facilities about every five years. This investment tax credit will be credited to that portion of the plant that is built in the future years, and that is going to influence the income stream in that future time as long as the growth is maintained at its present high rate.

Brasfield: That is assuming that Congress does not change the investment tax credit laws next year.

McCreath: Yes, we are assuming this is a permanent law, and it is going to be on the books for a long time—that is, it is going to be on the books as a law until it is changed, as Mr. Martin said. So we feel it does have a bearing.

Welch: But you are talking about taxing property that has not even been built yet, aren't you?

Fisher: No.

McCreath: No.

Reeves: No.

Fisher: All we are trying to do is quantify the income stream.

McCreath: I have always understood that either the FPC or the FCC regulations require the handling of the investment tax credit on a flow-through basis.

Coffey: No, that has all changed. There have been many misunderstandings concerning congressional intent with respect to the Code changes in 1969 and 1971. However, the 1975 changes, as well as the House and Senate Conference Reports, leave no doubt that normalizing is required for rate-making purposes. It would appear that the 1971 changes might have required this beginning in 1972.

Fisher: No, I thought there was something a great deal more recent than that— that they were going to insist on flow through of the investment tax credit, not on deferred federal income tax. That is an entirely different item. Now for investment tax credit, I understand that it is essentially all flow through at the present time.

Coffey: No, it is just the opposite.

Reeves: The National Association of State Regulatory Agencies has passed a resolution in opposition to the FPC rule requiring the investment tax credit to be flowed through. The FPC went flow through. The FCC went the other way.

Coffey: And the Internal Revenue Code also requires normalizing.

Reeves: Jim Martin, have you signed off on this or would you like to comment further?

Martin: No, I really have not come to any decisions on this particular question.

McCreath: Well, I would like to come back now to the second half of my original question. How many practitioners are doing what with this investment tax credit?

Coffey: You mean, how many are using flow through, and how many are normalizing? In Kentucky, and I will speak for Kentucky, they are normalizing.

Fisher: In Oregon, we are using flow through.

O'Brien: In Minnesota we are treating it as recommended by FCC and FPC.

Morrison: We are doing the same thing in Montana.

Franzman: We are doing the same in Arizona.

Reeves: How about Kansas?

McDougall: Well, since I am not a practitioner, I will not speak for Kansas.

Reeves: Bob McSwain, what do you do in Alabama?

McSwain: We use the flow-through method, but I think there is a great deal more to the question than we have covered. It is not enough to say that it is handled this way every place, but I think it depends on whether it is a company regulated by the FPC or other regulatory commissions. I would imagine the state regulatory commissions would be inclined to take the viewpoint that any savings in income taxes through the investment tax credit would have to be passed along to the consumer, so it is my feeling that the state regulatory commissions would handle things differently than the Federal Power Commission. They would order a reduction in rates, so there is no benefit to the potential purchaser as the credit simply results in a reduction in rates. I am not going to comment on the motivation of the state regulatory commissions, but they take the attitude that the utility company should not benefit from the federal income tax laws and that the ultimate beneficiary should be the utility customer or the consumer. They order a reduction in the stated cost of the installed plant that goes into the rate base and thereby reduce the actual rates to the users. So, I think the question really boils down to whether or not there is a benefit derived from the investment tax credit, and if there is a benefit to the company, then somebody is willing to pay for that benefit, and it is our job to find out how much. If everything flows through the consumer, obviously there is no benefit to the purchaser of the utility and there is no value attached to that particular item. I think that is the crucial point to the whole argument.

Welch: I would certainly agree with that point of view.

Reeves: You would use flow through, then, for estimating property values for property tax purposes in Alabama?

McSwain: That is right, if it is a benefit to the company.

Fleming: In Tennessee, we include it as an expense—that is, as an income tax item—and it is normalized. And we have the situation that parallels the one Bob was talking about where our commissioners on strictly intrastate companies look at it as an interest-free loan. They say they are not going to let the companies benefit from it because it is a one-time shot. On a $200 million plant, there is a $20 million investment tax credit, and the commissioners take the attitude that it should flow through to the benefit of the consumer.

Fisher: But that is not a loan.

Fleming: They treat it as a loan because it amounts to $20 million they did not have to spend—that is, $20 million they did not have to pay in income taxes.

Fisher: They never do have to pay it.

Fleming: That's right. It is just given to them right there, and the federal government is saying you have $20 million that you don't have to pay, and our utility commission says the rate payers need to receive the benefit of that $20 million and not the company.

McSwain: That is the way our commision handles it in Alabama.

Fleming: Our commission says if you are going to build on a $200 million plant, it is only going to cost you $180 million because you have $20 million in investment tax credit; then all you are going to be allowed to earn on is the $180 million net cost to you. So the consumer is the one who is going to benefit and not the company. Or we could do the equivalent thing and simply put that $20 million in as interest-free money on which the company would not be allowed to earn anything so it effectively is a zero rate of return on $20 million worth of debt. In Tennessee we handle the investment tax credit the same way we handle deferred federal income tax for rate-making purposes on intrastate companies.

Coffey: I would like to come back to the panel for a minute and ask the three gentlemen, do you think that if you were to invest $200 million in a new generating plant, you would automatically receive $20 million investment tax credit income? That is what you say when you use flow through.

Reeves: You did not have to pay that money out.

Coffey: But you certainly did not make any money on the transaction.

Fisher: If you have these big plant investments in any given year, they are just big surges, and what we do in Oregon to try to even things out is to take off those big investments that may occur in any one year. But where we can see a consistent pattern of additions that may run, say, $100 or $200 million a year on a year-in and year-out basis, all we say is the stream of income is going to reflect the same consistency that additional investments reflects. But if some company comes along and builds a billion dollar nuclear plant, then there is going to be that great big surge or peak, and we certainly cannot regard that as typical and we do have to even things out. That is the sort of thing that is not going to be recurring every year. But for the run-of-the-mill type investment tax credit, we simply say that your stream of income has been enriched by the amount of the tax credit. That is really a little extra frosting on the cake.

Brasfield: You are in effect normalizing, but you really are not normalizing in the real sense of the word. What you are saying is that you are not taking the investment tax credit as income in the year in which it is generated, but you are spreading it over the entire life of the property that is installed.

Fisher: That is right. What we are doing is assuming there is going to be about this much investment tax credit each year in the future, and we are basing our valuation on that concept and I call it flow through.

Brasfield: It really is sort of a normalization as I see it.

Fleming: Could you make the same set of assumptions with a pipeline company?

Fisher: Yes, I think you could, if they are putting so many dollars in it every year consistently.

Fleming: If we look at recent history in Tennessee, we would see that most pipeline companies were installing new facilities all the time. If we made this assumption of continuing growth—that is, a consistent amount of new plant added year after year—we would be finding out now, at least in our area in Tennessee, that we were dead wrong, because new pipeline construction has come to a complete halt as far as the natural gas pipeline companies are concerned. That may be hindsight, but it should serve as a warning to us on other kinds of property.

Fisher: I guess it would not apply to pipelines because our area is about the same. They have built about all the pipelines they are going to build. But in your electric companies where they continue to expand generating capacity and transmission capacity and in your railroads where they continue to buy new cars and locomotives, there is going to be a continual amount of new investment. All we are saying is that their income stream has been enriched by the tax credit that Uncle Sam in giving them where their tax expenses have been substantially reduced.

Reeves: I think Lowell Harriss has something to say at this point.

Harriss: I have been baffled by this particular question. I am not an accountant, but it seems to me that any property is going to be worth about the amount the regulatory commissions will recognize as an earning base. If they insist that the tax credit constitutes a reduction in the installed cost of the plant and that the utility be allowed to earn only on a reduced amount, then the value for rate purposes is diminished by that amount. If that is all they are going to earn on, then it is my feeling the value for tax purposes is reduced by a corresponding amount.

Fisher: Up to now we have been talking about the stream of income that is going to be generated by the total integrated complex. I think also we have to give consideration to the cost approach.

Harriss: The stream of income for suppliers of capital will of course be larger than if they had to pay the income tax, other things being the same. But if that income is reduced by the reduction in the amount of plant on which the company is allowed to earn, I do not see any major benefit to the company or the purchaser of the company. Hence, the worth for property tax purposes will not be the purchase price, but that minus commission adjustment (in rate making) for the investment tax credit.

Woolery: This is probably Professor Oldman's question, and since he is not here to ask it, I will advance it. I suppose the reason behind the investment tax credit is to encourage new plant investment on the part of American industry. To what extent is the state or local property tax administrator frustrating the intention of the federal government by trying to tax away the incentive that industry or utilities would have to make new plant investment thereby increasing the property tax base? So, are state and local tax administrators really at cross-purposes with the intentions of the Congress in trying to tax away a benefit that the Congress is trying to bestow on industry as a way to get it to make the kind of new investment that our economy requires?

Martin: Probably, but so what?

Fisher: I would submit that Congress has been frustrating the state and local tax administrators.

Coffey: I believe the states of Oregon and Alabama are in violation of federal law. I think the 1972 change in the Internal Revenue Code specifically prohibits this type of treatment for the investment tax credit. I think we are going to hear more about the federal role when we start talking about the Railroad Revitalization Act. There is an Internal Revenue change made in 1972 that says any agency must accept the normalization of the investment tax credit, whether it be rate making or tax administration.

Reeves: I had occasion to do a survey about a year ago. This was for regulatory purposes, and I found that in most states there was the change from flow through to normalization, which in effect was following the FPC's rules and of course the rules and regulations of the Internal Revenue Service. Speaking of the IRS, I don't recall the exact figures, but I believe that the electric utility companies have been paying very little actual taxes in the last few years, and I think that is brought about because of the investment tax credit and the deferred federal income tax that comes about because of the accelerated depreciation taken on this kind of property. I think two or three of the companies operating in the most populous areas of Kentucky pay no income tax because of the two mechanisms that we have just talked about. It seems to me that the nationwide figures show something like only 30 percent of the investor-owned utilities in the United States actually pay any income tax. So that is my comment about electrical utilities. I don't know about telephone companies and other utility properties. What is actually happening here is that we are allowing them credit for income taxes that are not paid. I don't know what this whole discussion is illustrating except that maybe the wisdom of what Ron Welch suggested—that is, to capitalize income before income tax.

Welch: Then we would have to ask the question: What kind of an income tax component do we put into the cap rate? We wouldn't really escape the problem by doing that.

Fisher: Yes, you have to answer the question: Is it 48 percent, is it 42 percent, or 5 percent, or 0?

Coffey: Clyde, I think that we had various pipeline companies in Kentucky that had built plants and had created quite large investment credit amounts. I believe in this case it would be incorrect to say they would not have paid any income tax on their earnings in the current year.

Reeves: I think one of them would anyway.

Coffey: I think they all would pay some income tax. But let's carry this point a little further. What about the accounting for the investment credit item for railroads and industry that just don't pay any income tax at all? I know Dr. Martin is involved in this, and I am sure that Don Fisher and Bob McSwain can help enlighten us on this item also.

Reeves: If a company is unfortunate enough not to make any money, it is penalized.

Fisher: Because it has no income to take the credit against.

Reeves: That is right.

Fisher: There is a very good example in the air transportation industry where it is common practice to rent or lease a whole fleet of planes. The airlines get this investment tax credit even though they are not making any earnings. So essentially the air transport industry is getting the tax credit through more favorable lease terms on its rented equipment because the owner of the airplane gets the credit and then returns the benefit to the airlines in the form of reduced lease payments. This cuts down on your operating expenses and improves your overall financial picture.

Reeves: I think there is something bothering Clarence Brasfield, so let's find out.

Brasfield: I would like to ask one question. Assume we are going to capitalize net operating income, and let's say there is $10,000 of net operating income that would go to a prospective purchaser. That is what he would anticipate receiving. Let's assume that the $10,000 in net operating income is arrived at through the method prescribed by the regulatory authorities—that is, by normalization of all deferred taxes, normalization of the deferred federal and state income taxes, and also the investment tax credit. After this normalized tax expense, we have $10,000 of net operating income. Now that is $10,000 that is available to pay the creditors and the equity owners, so we are going to build a capitalization rate with just those two components in it. We are assuming this is all the prospective owner is going to get—just the income that the regulatory procedures have prescribed.

Now assume that $4,000 of this $10,000 goes to pay interest—that is, it goes to the creditors of the business for the use of their money. Let's assume that the management has established a policy of total payout—no retained earnings but paying out everything left to the equity owners. We have $10,000 to pay out, so $4,000 goes to the debt holders and $6,000 goes to the equity owners. That takes care of the entire $10,000 of net operating income. Now if you go back and start fooling around with the regulatory accounting methods with regard to the normalization of federal income and investment tax credits, you may decide that instead of $10,000 in net operating income that there is $12,000 in net operating income. You are saying that the income tax expense item is not as great as has been shown and therefore there is $12,000 available to pay out in this example. My question is: Where does the company get the extra $2,000 to actually pay out to somebody?

Fisher: You get that because you booked more income tax than you actually paid, so you booked $2,000 more in expense than you actually paid out in cash expense and that left you the extra $2,000.

Brasfield: But the prospective purchaser is tied to the accounting rules of the regulatory authorities and the regulatory authority method of bookkeeping shows $10,000 as new operating income available for the debt and equity holders.

Fisher: That is what I said, it is per book, but not as an actual fact. What is the difference between this and the regulatory body allowing you so much depreciation on book value? You may book $10,000 worth of income, but actually you have a great deal more cash flow than that.

Brasfield: It seems to me this is an intangible item, and not anything that we can put our hands on.

Fisher: No, it is right in your cash account. You have got it. It is in your hand. Your bookkeeping shows $10,000 as net operating income, but if you go to your treasurer, you will find that he has $12,000 in cash in his cash account.

Brasfield: So what you are saying is that even though your books show only $10,000, you are suggesting that you could go to your treasurer and he could pay out any amount that you wanted.

Fisher: That is at your pleasure, depending on how you want to disperse the funds that you had in the bank.

Brasfield: But I don't have the discretion of deciding that I'm going to book it this way but that I am going to handle the money another way.

Coffey: You couldn't pay out the $12,000 in interest and dividends. I think you would be in violation of the law. You could only pay out the $10,000.

Martin: That is what I think, too.

Coffey: So wouldn't that be all that the investor could be looking at?

Martin: Yes, but keep the suspicious from thinking that it is a steal, and I am not taking a position one way or the other, but I think it is important that we do see the question in its proper light.

Fisher: You have one record for the treasurer, one record for IRS, one record for bookkeeping, and you may even have another record for stockholders. In fact, the railroads just changed a few years ago to more clearly spell it out in the stockholders report. I can remember discussions going back as far as 1954 with Union Pacific about not showing deferred federal income tax when they had defense plant certificates. Eventually they did show it in the stockholders report.

McSwain: Clarence and I talked about this for about 1,000 miles the other day, and I could not convince him in that 1,000 miles, but I agree with you, Don, that bookkeeping shows $10,000, but actually have $12,000 on hand in your cash account. But because of certain regulations, you might have to plow that extra $2,000 back into the business and not pay it out in dividends. The facts are the books do show you have $10,000 in net operating income, but if you went to the cash drawer you would find you have $2,000 more in cash or a total of $12,000. This occurs because even though normal IRS income tax procedures say you owe $4,000 in income tax and they allow you to deduct that from your books, actually they charge you only $2,000. So even though you have deducted $4,000 for bookkeeping purposes, you have only paid out $2,000, and you have an extra $2,000 left in your cash account.

Brasfield: Suppose that the bond rating agencies are looking at your financial statements, what are they going to consider when they start calculating the times interest charges earned for your actual interest coverage? Are they going to use the $10,000 on your books or the $12,000 in your cash drawer?

Fisher: I think you put your finger on the reason we are going to have two separate definitions of *times charges* earned in the new glossary we are going to publish—that is, interest coverage. One is after income tax and one is before income tax. I am sure the people have taken both into consideration.

Inflation's Effect on Value

Brasfield: I would like to add another dimension here and talk about the role of inflation in the kind of appraisal work we are talking about—how it affects valuation. Since we are talking about capitalizing earnings, I would like to pose this example. Five or ten years ago our cost per telephone was about $100, let's say for purposes of a single example, and now because of inflation, to replace that same plant would cost about $120. But we are allowed to earn on the historic cost, so our income for the older equipment does not actually go up to conform to the present-day replacement cost value of the new equipment that we are installing. When computing the income approach, at least in some states, it has been traditional to take five years of earnings and adjust them for the current plant level on the basis of change of investment over that period—that is, if you have a 50 percent increase in the investment you would increase the base year's income by 50 percent to bring it up to the current plant level. Now I find a lot of assumptions with this kind of an income stream adjustment because you are assuming that if you had had 50 percent more investment that year, you automatically would have had 50 percent more income. I think the problems of attrition and regulatory lag are such that that is not a valid assumption. So my real question is: How can you take those past years earnings and properly adjust them to reflect future potential earnings that you are capitalizing into an estimate of the present worth of the plant?

Reeves: I think that is something that Ron Welch might have touched upon previously, and perhaps he will comment on that now.

Welch: Of course, we all know there is such a thing as regulatory lag. Commissions do not instantaneously react to rate and rate base increases requested by companies, so it may be quite some time after equipment is installed before the regulatory agency actually allows increased earnings. I would say you would have to make your future estimates with full knowledge that there might be such a thing as regulatory lag and temper those estimates accordingly.

Reeves: Probably you could solve the problem by just capitalizing the current income and then add on at the bottom your construction work in process.

Brasfield: I don't think so. That just further expands the income stream from what I am talking about and does not really get to the problem because I am just talking about what is being earned on the operating property.

Reeves: You are valuing just the operating property. If you use only the income from operating property, which is capitalized, you are not using the income that would be earned on future property and you are not valuing construction work in progress at all through the capitalized earnings approach. The value is there, but I think you should add it back at the end.

Brasfield: That is not exactly the question we are talking about. What I am talking about is the practice of, when making the 1976 appraisal, taking a look at the income and the plant for 1975, 1974, and 1973 and computing the ratio of the plant in each of those years to the 1976 plant and then factoring up the income for the individual years by the difference in plant investment.

Reeves: If you are asking me what I think about that practice, I think it is nonsense.

Brasfield: Nonsense or not, it is still being used.

Martin: I think there is legitimate objection that any taxpayer might have to that particular procedure. However, the one Clyde has outlined does not have the same built-in objection, and if you simply add the actual cost of the construction work in progress at the end of the appraisal, after you have capitalized the current income, then you do not have the particular problem that you raised.

Brasfield: I think that the construction work in progress question is really a separate one from the particular question I asked, which had to do with factoring up previous years' income by taking the ratio of the plant in the year in which the income was produced to the current plant account and increasing income by that ratio.

McSwain: May I comment on that, Clyde?

Reeves: Yes.

McSwain: What we are really trying to do is anticipate the future income stream that this property will produce. You do not have a crystal ball, so you cannot look out into the future. The best indication of what the future holds will have to be based on what the past has shown. I think you can look at two to three years that have gone past as Clarence has said, and if the company is a rapidly growing company like one of the Bell System companies, the plant three years ago would have been considerably less than the current plant. I think that a good way of testing the validity of your income estimate for the future is to take the current plant over the plant in the previous year and take that factor times the income for that previous year to see whether you come up to the current income. If that projected income is greater than the current income, then you know that there is some regulatory lag and you are able to identify or measure it. Once you have tested the current income against the previous years incomes factored up by the plant ratios, you can decide whether your current income is proper in use for projecting future income. I think then you can talk about adjusting for construction work in progress. But the really important thing is the estimation of future income. Kentucky uses a method that is a weighted average where the current year is given a weight of five and the previous year of four and the previous year to that of three and the one previous to that two and the fifth year back at one. These are just tools to help make reasonable projections of future income.

Investor Actions and Attitudes

Franzman: I would like to get back to some of the things that we have been talking about, and one of them is investor expectation. Our objective in this business is to find market value. Dr. Bonbright indicated he doesn't care for fair market value but is looking only for market value. We do look to the market for information about that value in terms of the actions of someone who is actually investing. My inquiry is what does the investor really expect, and how does he go about making his investment decisions? We talked about the investment tax credit. How does the investor view that item? To me that is more important than how the FPC or the IRS treats it. Maybe the investor is looking at a different information than either one of those two agencies. My question relates to that and appendant to it is another question that my staff keeps asking me. When you capitalize income, we find an indicator of value that is usually substantially less than the cost indicator of value, particularly the original cost and often the net book. This is not disturbing by itself, but it raises the question of the advisability of making continuing investment in this particular enterprise or industry, if there is that much obsolescence in the industry as measured by the difference between the income approach and the cost approach. Why then do the investors continue to pour money into it? Are we doing something wrong in the appraisal process that makes the values arrived at through the capitalized earnings approach all substantially below the value estimates produced by the other two approaches?

Reeves: Dr. Bonbright, you were listening to that with a great deal of interest. Would you like to respond?

Bonbright: Yes, because I think that is a very important question. We must ask ourselves what actually motivates investors to decide on a particualr investment that is in competition with all other investments. When I read the writings of the investment analysts and when they are looking at this or that stock compared to other stocks, I find they are usually talking about "total return" on investment. That revolves around what dividend you can anticipate plus what increase in the market price of the shares of stock you can expect. I think the main emphasis as far as analysts are concerned is on market price. When you get right down to it, why does somebody pay $50 for a share of stock today? The answer is because it expects it to go to $55 in the near future. Now he hopes to get some current income from the dividend, but he also hopes to get his investment *more than returned* through appreciation in share prices. I think there is some pretty significant literature that supports the view that the market is the best test of real value—better than the estimates of the investment analysts. Perhaps a better test would come from what the insiders are doing, but that information is generally not available to outsiders. Finally, the valuation technique to determine what is sometimes called intrinsic value is best developed by Graham and Dodd in their distinguished treatise on "Security Analysis."

Reeves: Ron Welch, do you want to comment on this?

Welch: I think a fundamental question in valuation goes back to Richard Goode's master's degree work at the University of Kentucky in which he used past earnings compared with present prices to find capitalization rates, fully aware that past earnings may not tell exactly what future earnings are going to be. But how do you probe the minds of investors to find out their expectations of future earnings? There is one thing that you do know. You can put your money into a savings account and get a guaranteed return of around 7 percent on your investment at today's interest rates. So you can be pretty sure that when you see people investing in things that are less safe than savings accounts, they must expect to get a return greater than 7 percent, and the question is how much greater. I don't think there is any easy answer to that question. You can find some corporations that are sufficiently stable so you can say that a relationship of their earnings to the price people are paying for their stock is probably a good indication of what people expect as a return on their investment.

I would like to respond to a question that Seth Franzman raised—that is, why do people keep putting investment money into a corporation that is not making money? I think the answer is that what they put into the business in the past is sunk, but they may be able to make a profit on what they add to it. They cannot make that sunken capital earn, but they may be able to make money on the additional investment.

Reeves: Jim Martin must have something to add.

Martin: I would like to take a shot at the question just raised, and that was the question about the relationship of value to historical cost. Of course, it is partly answered in Ron Welch's comment about the historic cost being sunk, but you would add new investment in the hope of making a profit on it.

Sometimes you do have to throw good money after bad simply because the bad money has already gone to the dogs. When I was commissioner of revenue for the state of Kentucky, one of the tax representatives of the Illinois Central Railroad gave me a beautiful example of that. After the war, he indicated, it became necessary, in order to deal with the transportation problem of Illinois Central, to increase very substantially the size of the locomotives. This was before we had moved to nearly 100 percent diesel locomotives. He was doing a commentary on a bridge they had to build over the Ohio River to enable a locomotive between Chicago and New Orleans to get across because the old bridge would not support the new locomotives. He said, "We've got a good railroad from here to the Ohio River and a good railroad from the Ohio River all the way to New Orleans, and we can accommodate the points in between; but, if we cannot get our trains across the Ohio River, the whole thing is worthless." And since we are not making any profit, what excuse do we have for spending a lot of money for a bridge across the Ohio River? We are having to make a new investment when we are not even earning a return on what we already have. So what he said was, we have got to put some good money into that bridge or all of our previous investment on both sides of the river that we have already sunk is going to be completely worthless. We just cannot compete with the modern railroads unless we provide some facilities for getting our new locomotives across the Ohio River. The old locomotives that we have are outdated and worn out. So we are in a real pinch.

I think that is a good illustration of what Ron just said about the previous investment being sunk and the necessity for new investment in order to have a prospect of making a profit on it and at least retaining some value in the old plant.

But to get to the other point, it seems to me that public utilities are not different from the other classes of property and that historical cost is no guide to current values of any sort. That is just as true of public service corporations as it is of farm buildings or downtown property. It would be most unusual if there were much demand for the kind of facility that you built forty years ago. Most of these structures are obsolete, and there is little demand for them. Very few farm buildings, office buildings, or commercial plants are worth anything near their historic cost after a long span of years, and I think that public service corporations are in the same boat. You simply cannot expect to find any relationship between historic cost and market value after a long span of years.

Now there is another factor that is somewhat different, but it has been operating all along, and that is the inflationary spiral that has added the complication of changes in the value of money to get present values even farther away from those that we might have had in the past. I don't think you have any right to expect that there will be any kind of a reasonable or rational relationship between historic cost and current market values.

Bonbright: Dr. Martin, would you not qualify that just a little bit with respect to a utility property located in a state in which the regulatory commission uses original cost rather than replacement cost as a measure of the rate base?

Martin: No sir. Look at the railroads for example. For a long time the railroads had a monopoly. In the 1930s they did not make any money and came up to a point where they were not worth anything. Of course, at the same time there was competition arising and that helped make a big difference also. Of course, in the 1930s the railroad values would have suffered first from the depression that hit us and the competition that was gradually coming in from truck lines and other types of transportation. I think there is another factor in the valuation situation that needs to be emphasized, and this relates to the power companies and the telephone companies—that is, the effectiveness of the regulatory bodies is really quite overstated.

Bonbright: I think one of the effects has been the impaired financial status of the Consolidated Edison Company.

Martin: That does not make me think they are particularly effective because it is just as much ineffective to ruin a utility company by regulatory procedures as it is to allow a utility company to get away with the flag.

Bonbright: I suppose that you are using "effective" in the correct sense as "effective" for the purpose for which it was designed, and I am using "effective" in the loose sense of being influential.

Martin: I will agree that regulation is influential, but I think it falls far short of meeting its intended purpose.

Reeves: I would like to rearrange Professor Bonbright's question a little bit. Take the case of electric utilities or telephone companies. Most of the property they have is relatively new and quite useful and they are experiencing growth. In the case like this, wouldn't cost less depreciation or, I should say, replacement cost less depreciation be a useful criterion?

Welch: Using replacement cost less depreciation changes things a great deal because replacement cost is a long way from historical cost.

Martin: I think there you can get some approximation of reality, but the problem is you are not going to get from that replacement cost figure any indication of the relationship between historic cost and current market value. This is the question that was posed, and it is the one I was addressing.

Welch: I am incredulous. I cannot believe that either one of you mean what you say because I think it is generally the practice around the country, although I know there are some exceptions, to use historical cost less depreciation as the rate base. How can you go above this if historic cost less depreciation is the rate base on which earnings are predicated? Granted, you can go above it under some circumstances that Dr. Martin and Dr. Bonbright might have been talking about, but those occasions are relatively few, and the amount of deviation is relatively small. It is almost axiomatic that a property subject to rate regulation cannot be worth much more than its rate base.

Martin: I think that is a very big "if."

Welch: I don't think it is right now. Under the current situation, a lot of companies are not even earning on their existing rate base because of regulatory lag, so I would say that generally the current value would be something less than the rate base and would certainly be far, far less than reproduction cost less depreciation.

Bonbright: Could we come closer to agreement if we were to set original cost as an approximate upper limit to the value?

Welch: I would not want to establish it as an upper limit, but it may represent an approximation of the upper limit to value. Market value could, however, be far, far below it. The railroads, of course, represent an entirely different group. They are not regulated on a rate base anymore, so the regulatory activity does not relate to any of their cost elements as I see it.

Bonbright: I have not done too much comparing of the selling prices of stocks with their book values, but I have the impression that recently utility stocks have been selling generally a little bit under their net book value.

Reeves: I think that Dr. Bonbright is right. A good many utility stocks are selling below book value, but isn't this just a happenstance and shouldn't we really note that book value does not have any necessary relationship to market value?

Welch: I think there is a relationship. Book value relates to rate base, which relates directly to market value.

Bonbright: Suppose somebody wanted to estimate the market value of Commonwealth Edison stock. Suppose he wanted to determine whether it is a good buy at the present price. I don't think any analyst would be justified in ignoring the book value of the property in providing investment analysis.

Reeves: I doubt whether any expert analyst would be governed in any way by the book value when making his recommendations.

Bonbright: When you say "governed by," I assume you mean he at least takes notice, but is not necessarily guided by it.

Reeves: That is right. He mentions it, but is certainly not guided in his recommendation by the book value figure.

Welch: He would not automatically say, "This stock is selling for less than value; therefore buy it." But he would certainly want to know how the current price relates to book value.

Bonbright: He would be pretty worried if the stock were selling at 100 percent over book value because that would be a pretty abnormal situation, wouldn't it?

Brasfield: But wouldn't the analyst be concerned if the company continued selling new issues at less than book value over a long period of time? Wouldn't the existing shareholders be concerned about the deterioration of their equity position within the company?

McSwain: I am inclined to agree with Ron that book value does have some meaning, but I am not sure it has the importance that people once attributed to it, and I don't think that replacement cost has any meaning in the value of utility property. I think the definition of replacement cost is that of replacing the existing plant with one of like utility or function. That brings us back to the appraisal principle of substitution that says that no property is worth more than the cost of acquiring an equally desirable substitute, assuming no undue delay. When we look at a telephone company or gas company, we have no alternative. We must acquire the particular property that exists because there is no substitute property. I think that the very definition of replacement cost rules out its use in the valuation of regulated public utilities.

Martin: I agree with that. If I have given any impression that I believe to the contrary, then it was certainly not my intention to do so.

Measuring Loss in Value Due to Obsolescence

McSwain: I think one of the problems is that people do not recognize all the things you need to consider in the cost approach. You could throw out the cost altogether in railroads, but on the other hand, I could take the Frisco railroad last year and work out my cost approach on what I consider to be acceptable appraisal principles. Then after I complete my cost approach, I lay it aside and start working on the income approach. Then I finish the income approach, put it aside, and go to work on the market approach. When I finish, I turn all three pages up and look at my answers. In this case, the variation between the highest and lowest indicator of value was less than 5 percent, and I used all three approaches to value.

Welch: Did you use the Dubielzig method of modifying the cost?

McSwain: Yes I used the Dubielzig method for estimating obsolescence. I have heard that described, I think by John Gronouski, as being an incestuous operation, but I disagree with him. I think that it is a very useful tool.

Reeves: I think Ken Morrison has something he would like to inject at this point.

Morrison: I have some questions in my mind about obsolescence. I don't want to just throw out a general question, but I would like to hear some discussion on estimating obsolescence. I know Bob McSwain employs the blue-chip method— that is, he has some blue-chip railroads and compares the subject property on several different indicators with the same indicators for the blue chips. In that way he is able to arrive at an estimate of the percentage of obsolescence in the subject property. Of course, California's method is not to use cost approach at all, so it does not even become a factor at least as far as railroads are concerned. Oregon uses percentage of obsolescence, and I think Idaho stated it used weighted factors for getting its obsolescence factors. In Montana we have been switching from one to the other each year to find something that looks good. So I would like to hear just a general discussion about obsolescence, both functional and economic.

Reeves: Who would you like to have lead off on that discussion?

Morrison: Probably Ron Welch, if he would.

Welch: I have already stated my opinion. I don't think the cost approach is worth anything in valuing properties where there is substantial obsolescence, whether it be economic or functional. My inclination is to go directly to the income approach or the stock-and-debt approach and forget all about the cost. You cannot measure obsolescence except by the income approach or with stock-and-debt approach, so why fiddle around with the cost approach? I agree with Gronouski on the subject of incest as he applied the word to the determination of obsolescence by the "blue-chip" comparison method.

Martin: I will go along with that.

McCreath: I would like to inject a question here: What if your income is a negative factor before you get down to property and income taxes and investment tax credit and so forth? Then what do you do?

Welch: Before interest?

McCreath: Yes.

Welch: It is worthless property. Of course, it does depend upon the future, but if the past income represents the future, I think the property is worthless.

Martin: As one tax commissioner put it before the National Tax Conference several years ago, "When you have a railroad like that, you appraise it at zero and put it on the books accordingly."

McSwain: But, of course, we are faced with the problem of finding taxable value for the property, and we can't just write it off. I think the minimum value would be its scrap value.

Martin: I think that is right if the owner has authority to sell scrap.

McSwain: We made an appraisal of some property in Tennessee that we valued at scrap value. We had quite an argument because the tax representative was arguing that it was worth a whole lot less than scrap.

Martin: I think that we have to look at the problem of nonearning properties in light of some of the things Ron Welch said earlier, and that would be valuing a property whose end or termination is in sight. I can remember we had a problem of this type in Kentucky back in 1936. It involved a small pipeline that the owner said would be liquidated at some future date, and they were making preparations for that liquidation already. When we checked everything they had reported, we found out it was accurate in every respect, and all the evidence pointed up the fact that if the pipeline were allowed to remain in place, they would not get anything for it. We made a provision to write it off over a two- or three-year period, and then at the end of that operating period, we would simply put salvage or scrap value on what was left. By that I mean net salvage—that is, the cost of recovery and sales would be deducted from the actual price they would get for the scrapped assets. I think that is what Ron Welch meant.

Welch: Of course. Every generalization has to be qualified in some respect.

Harriss: I agree with you on the point of salvage value, but let's suppose you have an operation that is losing money and you cannot go out of business, you can't scrap it, and you can't have any salvage value. What is the value of a business that loses money year after year but is forced to remain in operation? Then it would appear to me that the property has negative value and not even any positive scrap value.

Martin: That is exactly what my friend in Mississippi was talking about. He was talking about a railroad that had no earnings but was forced to stay in operation because of the regulatory authorities. We did not have that kind of a legal requirement on pipelines in Kentucky in 1936, and that is why we were able to do what we did with that small pipeline.

Welch: Of course, we have to recognize when we are talking about future income we are talking about cash flow, not income after depreciation or what we would call a net operating income figure.

Reeves: Professor Bonbright, do you have any comment on obsolescence of this type?

Bonbright: It seems to me that as far as rate-making purposes are concerned, the total depreciation should be considered—that is, the actual physical deterioration plus the various kinds of obsolescence should be considered in the rate-making process. But I do not know of any utility regulatory commission that says, "We will take depreciation at some guideline figure and then add in an extra factor for obsolescence." It is my feeling that the regulatory body just takes a fixed amount each year of the historical cost and lets you write that off, or requires that you write that off, as depreciation. I guess they assume that includes the obsolescence.

Harriss: I think I have heard that Michigan employs a certain percentage of the ton-miles that railroads carry as an obsolescence factor.

Morrison: Yes, I think it is something like 500,000 ton-miles.

Harriss: That seems to me to be an awfully crude device. You ought to factor in some receipt element such as revenue per ton-mile in order to have a meaningful figure.

Bonbright: I suppose the rate at which deductions should be made for depreciation would depend on whether the depreciation is of an obsolescence character or not. If it is merely a shorter length of physical life situation, then it is merely a problem of adjusting the time period and allowing a little more each year. If property had a twenty-year life, you would treat it like a twenty-year annuity and recover so much each year.

Reeves: Ken Morrison, I hope you have had some help from all this.

Correlating the Three Approaches to Value

McSwain: If I may, I would like to say a few words about that topic also. When we look at railroad valuation, I am not really comfortable with any of the three approaches. I agree with Ron Welch that cost is certainly not a good indication of value, but I think you should at least look at it. It can be made meaningful to a certain extent. For most of the railroads, it is very difficult to get a meaningful stock-and-debt figure, so if we throw out cost and say it is no good and then look at stock and debt and throw it out too, all we have left is the income figure. If we say it doesn't really have any meaning because it is difficult to develop a capitalization rate, where does that leave us? You must make an evaluation, so we do the best we can with what is available to us. This is not unique to us because an appraiser is faced with many similar problems in the regular appraisal field. So I think you have to take each of the three approaches and try to get as much out of each one as you possibly can. We have had a certain measure of success supporting the cost approach by using what we call the Dubielzig system to measure obsolescence. In making any appraisal, you are supposed to employ generally accepted appraisal principles, and this technique seems to conform with appraisal principles when you compare the subject property to some definite yardsticks. If a fee appraiser were appraising a hotel or an apartment house, he would measure the obsolescence by similar technique. What we would do in estimating the obsolescence factor for a particular railroad is exactly what a fee appraiser would be doing in appraising a hotel or apartment property, so we can make a pretty good case for this type of comparison in establishing the amount of obsolescence. When we look at the income approach, we may have as many doubts about it as we have about the cost approach, and the stock-and-debt approach will raise a similar series of doubts. When we look at the three approaches and try to correlate them to resolve some of our doubts, if they all seem to come back to somewhat the same level of indicated value, I feel a lot more comfortable with my final value estimate.

Bonbright: I think what you are saying, Bob, is that it is dangerous to say that something doesn't mean anything.

McSwain: That seems to me what I have been hearing here. People have been saying cost does not mean anything, and I say it does mean something. Of course, it may receive only a little consideration as far as its ultimate weighting in the appraisal is concerned. I say that each of the approaches has some meaning, but I may look at one of the approaches and decide not to pay much attention to it.

Fisher: I think what Bob says is important. There are a fairly large number of court cases that indicate you must consider all the evidences of value. Even though you may not give much credence to one particular approach, it is important that you have given it thorough consideration. Based upon that thorough consideration, you may decide to reject it completely, but then you are in a position to state that you considered it carefully and that you rejected it for good reason. So you have used it, but only in a very limited sense.

Stock and Debt

Reeves: Seth Franzman, you had some question.

Franzman: I would like to clarify something that we talked about earlier. I may be raking over some dead coals, but this relates to stock and debt. Yesterday Dr. Martin said that stock and debt may no longer be a usable indicator of value. I would like to be sure that I understood him to say that was with regard to the valuation of railroad properties that are part of a conglomerate and not utility properties in general where the operating corporation's principal business is the utility operation.

Martin: I don't think I went so far as to say that stock and debt is useless because I don't think that it is yet. But I think that its usefulness is diminishing. I think that is especially true in the case of railroads, and that is the situation that is developing in the case of truck lines also. But in the general utility operations, it is my feeling that we can still make some use of the stock-and-debt indicator of value. I think one of the best uses we can make of the stock-and-debt method is to help us develop better capitalization rates rather than using the stock-and-debt indicator as a pure valuation figure. Because when we use it as the capital value in relation to earnings in order to develop a capitalization rate, we are using averages of several companies, and one at least stands a chance of having compensation for error in both directions—that is, the offset of negative and positive factors should bring you back to good middle ground. And, even when the number of companies is as limited as it is, you have a chance to come up with some reasonable numbers. The other point you are making is correct. I was not talking about other classes of companies, but I think the evidence is accumulating that the stock-and-debt method is losing value for some other classes of property.

Bonbright: It is not quite clear to me why you are making those statements about the stock-and-debt method of valuation becoming useless. Would you explain why this is true, and especially in the case of railroad property? Is that because railroads are becoming more and more part of a conglomerate ownership in which the actual transportation property is being overshadowed by other types of enterprises that are not part of the railroad operating unit?

Martin: Yes, that is right. But there are really two big reasons. The first is that the industry is reorganizing in such a fashion that the stock of the operating company is not actually on the market. The stock of the parent company that holds all of the stock of the operating company is on the market, but the parent company really is not a railroad. The Chessy Corporation owns railroad stock, but it does not operate any railroads. The C&O stock, thus, is not on the open market. And that is one of the reasons I say the stock-and-debt method for valuing railroad property is losing utility.

Now, the other reason is the one that you suggest. Many of the railroad companies are getting so much property outside the operating unit that for assessment purposes particularly you cannot get an accurate elimination of that part of the business that is not the railroad business. In many corporations you have more income from nonrailroad business than you have from the actual railroad operation. The Santa Fe was in that position about ten years ago.

But in the case of that particular variation, we were fortunate in having good information about the nonoperating property, so we were able to do a stock-and-debt valuation that did lead us to a fairly good value estimate for that railroad operating property of Santa Fe Industries. But here we had good cooperation from the company, and the information was readily available to us. In the case of the Southern Pacific railroad, we had a great deal more difficulty in sorting things out, and I am sure the quality of our work was not as high as for the Santa Fe.

Welch: It has been my observation that engineers who have turned appraisers do not think that the stock-and-debt method of valuation is worth anything. They have a problem with the accounting theory that the liability side of the balance sheet is equal to the value of the assets.

Martin: There is one more thing that I should add here that is becoming more and more true. For instance, we have deferred federal income taxes accumulated on the liability side, and the question has to arise: What is the value of these deferred taxes to Uncle Sam or to whomever they are owed? In my opinion, there is no way of knowing under the existing situation. Not too long ago we didn't have that particular item, but now deferred federal income tax is a whale of a big item for a lot of our railroads. It is 25 to 30 percent, and in one case it was over 50 percent of the total liabilities other than the securities outstanding.

I think this is a very difficult situation, and it does distort the balance sheet because nobody really understands it. There are problems of the same nature on the asset side of the balance sheet, but in a different fashion and in a different direction.

O'Brien: I don't really have any questions as such, but there are a couple of items I would like to touch on. In Minnesota two of us have the primary responsibility for utility valuation, and our total experience in the field is about four years. Needless to say, I feel that in this company I am batting out of my league. We have been wrestling with our present method of valuing public utility properties for about two to two and a half years. In late 1975 we finally produced some values, and this year utility companies are paying taxes based upon those valuations. I thought we had a pretty good method worked up until I was exposed to the conversation of the last two days around this table. Now I feel I had better go back to Minnesota and get back to the drawing board again.

Allocating Value

Fisher: I would like to introduce a topic that may take some time to explore, but I think it affects everyone who is concerned with utility and railroad valuation. This problem involves allocation of the value once it is determined, especially for railroad equipment. In the railroad operation, we have two kinds of rolling stock: Railroad equipment that is owned by a common carrier railroad, a class 1 carrier by definition; then we have a second category of railroad equipment that is owned by private car companies. Of course, a private car company could be an owner/shipper or an owner/nonshipper.

In the case of private car companies, we resort largely to a wheelage or a car-mile allocation method, and we take as our factor the ratio of car-miles in the reported state to the amount for the total fleet in the entire country. In the case of railroads, I think substantially every state relies on the famous case of *Kentucky vs. Union Pacific*, which is discussed in the 1954 Unit Value Report. We think of the fleet of cars or locomotives as a hive of bees that go out in every direction, and we assume there is an equal interchange of equipment between the different carriers. So, we end up allocating a certain percent of the value of a carrier that operates in your state to your state to tax. We may say your state has 10 percent of the company's car-miles, so 10 percent of the rolling stock value is assignable to your state for assessment and taxation.

We now have an innovation that I am sure stems from IRS and the federal income tax rules and regulations. We are now encountering numerous switching companies and short-line railroad companies who operate 100 percent in one state. They will buy a fleet of anywhere from 500 to 1,000 cars and immediately throw them into the nationwide pool, which will then, through per diem or incentive rates, wind up in rental equipment. There is a 1962 court case in Pennsylvania that held that you cannot assess the total fleet in the state in which the fleet is domiciled, if it can be demonstrated that these cars are someplace else. But these cars that are someplace else will not be taxed by somebody else because they do not appear in the inventory of any reporting railroad. We have a company called The White City Terminal Utility Railroad Company down in southern Oregon. Its initials are WCTU. The WCTU railroad company bought five hundred cars and immediately threw them into nationwide distribution, putting them into the fleet all around the country on a lease-rental basis. They report no mileage in Oregon, and those cars are running on Union Pacific track, Southern Railroad, Illinois Central, and wherever, and they will never be reported to any state taxing jurisdiction. We recently received a bulletin stating that a Food Machinery Corporation, which has a big plant in Portland, had just sold somewhere between 500 and 1,000 cars to three different railroads. One is a little short-line railroad in Wisconsin, I think another is in Georgia, and the other is in Florida. There is getting to be a large number of these. Union Pacific could put all of its rolling stock into the little Mt. Hood Railroad, which is about twenty miles long and 100 percent in Oregon. U.P. could put its entire fleet into Mt. Hood Railroad and escape property taxation on it. Now the thing I am leading up to is this: How do you solve this problem of enormous amounts of railroad rolling stock escaping property taxation? I am convinced no state is going to receive reports from these short-line railroad and switching companies. Maybe we don't have jurisdiction over them. Maybe we will need statute changes so the state can assert jurisdiction over these companies or over any property that enters the state rather than any company that operates in the state.

Welch: Don, why don't you get 100 percent of the WCTU? I don't understand that.

Fisher: Because the case of the Central Railway of New Jersey against the State of Pennsylvania, which was settled in 1962, says you cannot do it. Our attorneys agree with that case, and we are now in the position of having to decide whether we are going to mount an attack on that particular case.

McSwain: I know the problem. In Alabama we have a twelve-mile railroad that has almost as many miles of cars as track. I have used the beehive theory in assessing it, and so far they have not appealed.

McCreath: Are you suggesting that these cars do not show up in the rolling car count or the standing car count in either case?

Fisher: That is about it. Each of these cars has established a taxable situs in nearly all of the forty-eight states in which we have continuous railroads running. But the company does not operate in the state of Idaho, so Idaho has no jurisdiction over it and it does not have to report to you. The company's cars may be there because they are used by the Burlington Northern or the Union Pacific, and you would not pick them up in your rolling car count because you are getting reports only from the parent or operating company, which is Union Pacific or Burlington Northern, and they just report what they own. They do not report everything that they use. Now the car-miles are there in the car-mile total versus the system total. But when you go to multiply this against some inventory, you are not multiplying against the inventory of the owning company. You are multiplying against the inventory that the operating railroad shows on its books, so the five hundred cars of the WCTU are tossed into the pool, but they are not accountable to anybody.

McCreath: But they would show up in the track count, wouldn't they?

Fisher: In the yard count you might catch them, but if you counted any WCTU cars, you would not try to tax them in Idaho since WCTU is a railroad company and not a private car company. Now the question is: Do you have the authority to assess a foreign railroad car owned by say Penn Central, Illinois Central, or Southern Railway if it shows up in Idaho?

McCreath: I don't believe we do.

Fisher: You haven't done this because there is presumed to be an equal interchange flowing back and forth from one carrier to another carrier. However, we have here a little switching company that is not a carrier. All it has done is enter into the private railroad car renting business, and it is going to escape substantially all of the property taxes.

McCreath: Don, what is the incentive that has led to the development of this type of company?

Fisher: The Association of American Railroads came out with new per diem and wheelage rates plus an incentive plan where they get extra special rent during certain seasons of the year. To the extent that a private invenstor can come in and just take these cars and make them available, he can get better utilization out of them than an operating railroad. I guess I really don't know what else is involved, but I have my suspicions that the federal income tax lies behind all of this activity. It may be that other railroads do not have enough reported income to take advantage of this sort of measure. The WCTU company is owned 100 percent by the Union Tank Car Company, and the Union Tank Car Company is owned 100 percent by Transunion Corporation, and the cars are leased from Walter E. Heller. WCTU rents these out to carriers, they are put into common carrier service, and that is how involved everything is.

Fleming: These cars are not permanently leased to anybody? They are different from cars that are on a permanent lease basis?

Fisher: No, they are not permanently leased; they are just part of the interchange, and they get paid the per diem and the mileage rates and the special incentives.

McSwain: This railroad I mentioned in Alabama has a company in California that owns the cars, and it leases them to this small local railroad and the railroad picks up the per diem. The California company gives the local railroad $6,000 a month to handle the accounts, and that is all it gets out of it—$6,000 a month.

Fisher: How many of these cars do you think are continuously in Alabama?

McSwain: Probably none.

Reeves: Do you tax them all in Alabama?

McSwain: Every one of them, under the beehive theory.

Fisher: Not under the beehive theory, because that would be zero. You are taxing them under the domicile theory.

McSwain: Yes, that is right. I am saying the beehive theory because we have the local railroad in Alabama and that is home base.

Fisher: You are saying that they are all in the hive. There may be some humor in this, but we have a serious problem. Do you assess five hundred cars in Oregon and say the U.S. Supreme Court does not understand the problem?

Book Value versus Market Value

Coffey: If it is all right with you now, I would like to play a new game, and I would like to address my remarks primarily to Dr. Bonbright. I would like him to assume the role of the chairman of the Securities and Exchange Commission for a moment, and I would like Dr. Martin to assume the role of senior partner in the accounting firm of Arthur Anderson & Co. I want you to imagine Bob McSwain is just finishing his testimony as the financial vice president of a railroad company before a hearing in which you are present. He testifies that the market value of his company's property is only $200 million, although the annual report to the stockholders shows the value of the company's assets to be $500 million. I would like to ask Mr. Bonbright, sitting as the chairman of SEC, if that would disturb him?

Bonbright: I assume that the $500 million figure is both in the annual report to the stockholders and in the report to the regulatory commissions.

Coffey: Yes.

Bonbright: I am not really acquainted with any situation in which the annual report to the stockholder undertakes to tell the stockholders what the physical assets of the company are currently worth. I am acquainted with the accounting entries that show a book figure that is for the most part the original cost less depreciation.

Coffey: Thank you. Now I would like to turn to Dr. Martin, who is playing the role of the senior partner of the accounting firm that has to attest to the balance sheet. Now he has just heard the testimony of an officer of the company to the effect that the assets of the company are really worth only 40 percent of what you certified them to be in the report to the stockholders.

Martin: Are you saying 40 percent of what is shown on the balance sheet?

Coffey: Yes.

Martin: That would not disturb me.

Coffey: You would still attest to the fact that it was a balance sheet showing $500 million?

Martin: Yes, if the facts indicated that figure, it would not bother me in the least.

Coffey: The problem seems to be a little more serious to me.

Fisher: Coleman, we have talked about this in years past, and maybe some of us who are appraisers do not appreciate how a CPA views the credibility of the stockholders' report that presumably is trying to portray what the assets are worth. I am sure the accountant has a far different viewpoint toward this than those of us who are lay people. I think that is a technical concern that bothers you because of your accounting background and your professional standing.

Coffey: Personally, I would not attest to the report. I would refuse to do it. I would think the SEC would have a greater charge than the independent accountant because of its responsibility to the public.

McSwain: I would imagine that you, as a CPA, have signed many reports where the value of the property is greatly in excess of what you attested to on the balance sheets.

Coffey: Yes, but never any lesser, to my knowledge.

McSwain: What is the difference, if it is greater or lesser? Actually you are only attesting to the fact that these books are kept in accordance with generally accepted accounting principles and that is entirely different than valuation. You are not attesting to value, whether the value be higher or lower than the accounting figure.

Coffey: Generally, accepted accounting principles, in my opinion, would represent the minimum value.

McSwain: You are not asked to make any valuation.

Coffey: Yes, I am.

McSwain: As an accountant?

Reeves: Aren't generally accepted accounting principles supposed to make some sense?

Coffey: No, not if regulatory controls restrict them to where they overstate values on the balance sheet.

McSwain: Sense from an accounting standpoint can be different from sense from a valuation standpoint. Take a railroad, for instance. With all the water in the railroad accounts and the railroad books, the total of the assets would be much greater than the actual value of that railroad; yet those annual railroad report statements are attested to by CPAs every day.

Coffey: If they are, then I think this is a terrible mistake—that is, if what you say is true. But I say I would not attest to any balance sheet if I knew for sure that the value of the assets was not equal to or greater than the amount stated on the balance sheet.

McSwain: Why lesser? Why not greater?

Fleming: If the assets were worth twice as much as the stated figure on the balance sheet, would you sign it then?

Coffey: Yes. It would not bother me. You make a reserve for bad debts, which you hope is adequate.

McSwain: There you are valuing only one small item, and that is in the accounts receivable. It is only in the area of receivables that an allowance or reserve is made on the balance sheet. All you have done in the fixed assets is to determine that you are going to recover them over a certain fixed period of time. It is quite possible that appreciation might exceed depreciation, but you do not take that into consideration.

Coffey: But if you use this attested balance sheet to go to a third party to borrow money or to go public, I think you would be in serious trouble.

McSwain: I cannot see your position that if it is higher it is all right, and if it is lower it is not.

Coffey: If it is higher, there is no danger.

Martin: Let me jump into this and see whether I can stir it up a little. Suppose that the transactions reflected in that balance sheet were concentrated, and this is just for the sake of argument, in the 1950s and 1960s. Suppose we are talking about this situation in the year 1976. Now the value of money has changed a great deal, and simply the changes in the value of money would make those figures much higher.

Coffey: Yes.

Martin: Now suppose you reverse that. Look at a situation like one that prevailed in 1934 as reflecting transactions that had taken place from 1910 to 1925. In 1934 the bottom had fallen out of the value of everything that was for sale, so there would have to be as much difference on the other side.

Coffey: Then I think the CPA has to determine what the market value is in 1934 if it is less than the stated book value.

Martin: That does not trouble me a bit. It is going to be less because of the change in the price level.

Coffey: But certainly there is no reason for the accountant to witness a taking of the inventory, and thereby verifying the pricing for a third party to make sure the value is there.

Martin: I don't think that is a problem for the accountant. He is dealing with integrity of the accounts from the standpoint of historic cost, taking depreciation into account. And that is where his obligation is. His obligation is not to give you a figure that represents market value as of a given date.

Fisher: Coleman, as a CPA, if they had a $1 million worth of internal supplies or inventory, and you find out they were worth say only $100,000, would there be a budget note or an accounting note, or would you reduce them down to the $100,000 figure?

Coffey: You would require them to write the value down, or you would refuse to attest.

Fisher: Would you apply this to accounts receivable, materials and supplies, any liquid assets?

Coffey: Any type of assets.

Fisher: You are saying this also applies to fixed assets.

Coffey: Certainly, where we have the situation of a company official who has testified that the value of the fixed assets are only worth 40 percent of the stated book amounts.

Fleming: But you are not required to write them up.

Coffey: No, you are not required to write them up.

Welch: Let me ask you this question, Coleman. What if the value of the property, looked at from an appraiser's viewpoint rather than an accountant's viewpoint, is less than the debt? The equity has been wiped out, and the deficit is such that you cannot even support the debt. Under those circumstances would you say that the corporation is precluded from declaring any dividend?

Coffey: Certainly, and I think that under the circumstances the independent auditor would not attest to the financial statement.

Welch: I am supposing now that you do write the assets down, but you write them down to less than the debt, so that you have a negative net worth.

Coffey: Yes that is not uncommon. You can attest to an opinion that states a negative net worth.

Welch: Are there any legal consequences that flow from this such as bankruptcy or receivership or restraint upon issuance of new debt or equity?

Coffey: I am sure there would be, and this is the reason I think the SEC would be involved.

Bonbright: I think it is important that we distinguish between the fixed assets and the current assets. It is the fixed assets that we have to book at their cost minus an allowance for depreciation, and that figure does not purport to represent their current value to be $50 million. It simply reports a matter of history—what it did in fact cost and what have been the depreciation charges ascribed to it. Years ago the head of the Accounting Department of the Columbia University School of Business made the statement that fixed assets ought to be booked at original cost, and then he made the further statement that the reason why they should be booked at original cost was that original cost represented value of the assets to the going concern. I think that was an erroneous statement. I doubt whether any modern book on accounting would assert that the reason why fixed assets are usually booked at original cost is that original cost represents the value of those fixed assets to the going concern. What it represents is the historical fact as to what the assets really did cost originally.

Coffey: I do not distinguish between fixed assets and working capital as far as attesting to the balance sheet is concerned.

Martin: Coleman, in the case of railroads, the rules of the Interstate Commerce Commission require that this be done exactly at Professor Bonbright has outlined. I think that it is good accounting practice too. I am talking about the fixed assets now.

Coffey: I feel as an accountant that I would not attest to a balance sheet if I knew that the fixed assets were not worth as much as the book figure.

Martin: You do not want to get in touch with the railroads on the accounting responsibility item because they could not go along with you and stay out of jail.

Fisher: I think Coleman is not questioning the railroad's report to the ICC, but he is questioning the report, which he has to certify to, that is going to the stockholders and to the public generally.

Coffey: That is right, and I am concerned with the SEC's role in protecting the investing public.

McSwain: Generally, that report has a few adjustments, but in most cases it conforms to the company's books.

Fisher: Those few adjustments are exactly what Coleman is talking about.

McSwain: No. What he is concerned with is the value of the assets—that is, the value of the fixed assets, part of which is represented by unearned surplus, and as a result, the figures are rather large, and that part is not adjusted in the report that goes to the SEC or the stockholders. The report that goes out and is signed by the CPA firm greatly inflates the value of the property of the railroads. And, as I said, these are signed by CPAs everyday.

Stability of Tax Base

Coffey: I am sure what you are saying is true, Bob. Let's move on to another thing about which I have some concern, and I would like to address the question to Dr. Martin and Dr. Bonbright again about the responsibility that we have in assessing public service company property, since in some states it makes up any-where from 10 percent to 60 percent of the total tax roll. How do we keep the fluctuations in value from year to year out of the tax base? How do we eliminate outside influences so we do not get these very wide fluctuations each year? And under the concept of defining market value, how far can we go in stabilizing these assessments on a year-to-year basis without being subject to being sent to jail for fraud or the like?

Bonbright: I think there is wisdom in making the valuations for tax purposes fairly stable, but there is no question that the value indicated by the stock-and-debt method and the capitalized earnings approach are going to change from year to year. I think the tax administrator has a certain obligation to consider the impact of these fluctuations on the tax base and perhaps make some adjust-ment for them. I think here you are asking us to form a conception of normal value in the Alfred Marshall sense of the word. But this, of course, is a very dif-ficult thing to bring forth, especially in the case of monopoly property, because in the Alfred Marshall sense of the word, value depended upon the existence of competition to develop a competitive price structure.

Reeves: The question here is: How much is the assessor justified in tampering with market value in the interest of stability of the tax base, because he has to be concerned both with the interest of the taxpayer and the interest of the taxing jurisdiction?

Welch: He should not be doing this at all. That is a function of the tax rate. If the tax rate has been so circumscribed by law that it does not work out right, then we should change the law.

Martin: I am in accord basically with that view, but I would make several obser-vations to the contrary. I think we are justified in some maneuvers that may bring about greater stability in year-to-year valuations for tax purposes. This may take the form of averaging past income to indicate future earnings instead of taking just one year's income for use in the income capitalization indicator of value. And in the stock-and-debt method, I think you could make a good case for a six-month or twelve-month average of stock prices and bond prices from quotations. These are the kinds of things that I think you can do legitimately as a tax administrator to help stabilize the tax base on a year-to-year basis. I still agree with someone who stated earlier that we are valuing the property as of now and that prior years really have nothing to do with it.

McDougall: It is interesting to me that yesterday we threw out everything except market value (including "fair" market value) and today we are back where we began talking about "stable" market value.

Reeves: I think we are talking about two different things. One is valuation and one is assessment.

McDougall: But Dr. Martin was talking about averaging income over a three-year period to derive a stable value indicator.

Reeves: Assessment.

McDougall: An estimate of value that may be then used for assessment. I would suggest the reason you take three years or five years or even ten years is not to get a stable estimate of value, but to get closer approximation of the future income, thinking that income one year has a random component, but that a five- or ten-year income stream would balance out to a normal or typical income figure. I think, however, that it is best not to eliminate stability since value is not stable. This is especially applicable if you look at the stock-and-debt approach. If anything is unstable, it certainly must be this because of the way share prices move up and down on the stock exchanges.

Martin: Historically, it really is not as bad as you may think. Frequently when stocks are going up, bonds are going down, and the increase in the value of equity side is offset by decreased value on the debt side. The same conditions pertain in the reverse.

Deferred Income Taxes

Fleming: I have one quick question, and then I want to come back to that matter of deferred federal income tax. I would like to ask Dr. Martin whether he excludes the deferred federal income tax from the income stream in the capitalized earnings method for railroads. I know you make several tests of the income stream at various levels, but in the last few years the ICC said that the deferred federal income tax must go in above the line instead of below the line where it used to be. I would like to get your viewpoint on this.

Martin: I don't think there is any right answer to that, except maybe putting it above the line. As Ron Welch said, that does not solve the problem, it just puts it in another place. I think it may be more practical to handle it in another place. We do it both ways, but when my theoretical knowledge flies in the face of the market, I must say that I withdraw my theoretical knowledge and I am guided by the market.

McSwain: I would like to ask Dr. Martin whether he thinks it would be reasonable to assume that deferred federal income tax is taken off as an expense, but in actuality it is something that will never have to be paid. A potential purchaser would be buying the actual income stream so it should be capitalized like any other income. The company will be able to use that money until accelerated depreciation runs out and you reach the crossover point where it will have to pay higher income taxes. Making that assumption, would it be reasonable to say that a potential purchaser would have use of this deferred federal income tax until accelerated depreciation falls below the amount that could be taken on a straight-line basis? Could we determine the value to someone who had the benefit of that extra money for a full fifteen-year period and then would pay back one-fifteenth of it each year for another fifteen years?

Martin: We do not know the answer to the question you posed. We do not know whether that will be repaid in the future or not.

McSwain: Right. But you have to make one assumption or the other.

Martin: No, you could split the difference.

McSwain: I don't know what the answer would be, but I have done some studies on this. What do you think, Ron?

Welch: What you proposed sounds pretty good to me. It seems to me that this is a liability that may never mature.

Fleming: I would like to get Don Fisher's opinion on this.

Fisher: I don't think the board of directors or the U.S. Congress or anybody else can say this is never going to be paid back to the U.S. Treasury. If they do, then it is immediately going to have the smack of a political boon-doggle, so we have to start off with the premise that it is going to be paid back sometime. Then it is just a case of discounting those future payments or future credits, whichever the case may be, to a present worth.

McSwain: So you are agreeing with my second idea.

Fisher: Yes.

Public Law 94-210

McSwain: I don't think that we can leave valuation without talking about Public Law 94-210,[a] which says that railroad proprerty subject to ICC regulation cannot be assessed more than 5 percent above the general assessment level for commercial and industrial property or taxed at a rate different from this property. It seems to me that we are going to have to sharpen up our total valuation bag of tools to be sure we have valued railroads and commercial and industrial property on the same basis.

Reeves: Based on our conversation so far, is there anybody here who feels he could assess a railroad within 5 percent of its true value?

Fisher: What is true value?

McSwain: Wouldn't "true" be in the same category as "fair" that we talked about before?

Fisher: I don't know, but I think this is going to force us all into a corner as administrators. I have noticed that over the past ten-year period in the western states at least, where we get together as tax administrators for various states and compare values, that our values are coming closer and closer together for the properties that are interstate in nature. I would say we are now within 5 percent or 10 percent as far as our valuations are concerned for most of the interstate properties in the western states. The allocation problem is another matter, but just by working together we learn from each other, and we have produced some well-equalized valuations.

Reeves: I can see some hazards in states going in on interstate property with separate states having very large valuation differences. Say one neighboring state is appraising a railroad at 50 percent more than the state next door. I think this could put us in a very weak position as valuers.

Fisher: I agree, and I think this is going to force us to work more closely together as state administrators on the valuation of interstate property.

McSwain: We have been moving together more closely in the southeastern part of the country, through our Southeastern Association of Tax Administrators, and generally there is less than a 5 percent difference in the valuation of interstate properties among the eleven or twelve states in the Southeastern Association of Tax Administrators.

---

[a] See Appendix D.

Brasfield: Wouldn't it be fair to say that as long as the states are getting together to work on uniformity in assessment of railroad property, that they also do likewise on all other property?

Valuation Research

Reeves: I would like to raise one issue before we go to the summary of what has been said, and that revolves about the kind of research that could be conducted into the valuation problems of public service corporations. I think we have a lot of unresolved issues, and certainly we have raised more questions than we have answered in this two-day conversation on valuation, but what particular questions that have surfaced in the last two days are really amenable to research? Once those are identified, what is the proper type of research effort to improve the valuation of public service corporations for assessment purposes?

Martin: In my judgment, most of these unanswered questions referred to by Clyde may lend themselves to research treatment. I think one of our first efforts should be in the direction of refining methods of developing improved capitalization rates. I would hope the early emphasis would be on determining the best capitalization rate for handling the operating property of railroads and later all other types of utilities. I really mean utility property generally, and we should not put any more emphasis on railroads than on other utilities—that is, power companies, pipelines, and communication companies generally.

I think another area that calls for considerable work and study is the area involving investment tax credits and the deferred federal income tax, and the role that these two items will be playing in our valuation estimates for public service corporations.

Another item we have not considered very seriously, but which I think is a very serious issue and particularly applies when dealing with the capitalization rate problem, is the change from accrual of dividends received by a reporting corporation to a scheme that covers, in addition, the reporting corporation's equity in the earnings of subsidiary corporations that were not declared as dividends and also in the losses to whatever extent they were incurred. The way this impinges on the capitalization process is that, number one, you have an accrual that never becomes a property in any sense of the word and then gets lodged in the balance sheet and becomes an asset item. That is what I would call a visionary asset, or imaginary would maybe be a better term, because it does not have any reality in the sense that it never will become a property of the parent corporation on whose balance sheet it is going to cause some distortions, and there are some corporations in which this has become a very large item.

Then, I think we should face up to the fact that undertaking research projects of this type is going to result in a certain amount of lost motion. Some of the problems we have been discussing just don't have any answers. But I still think the research must be undertaken. I don't think that any good researcher should turn down a project because he thinks there just isn't any answer to the question. I think that conclusions should flow from research.

Reeves: Maybe we could hear from Ron Welch.

Welch: I am not sure that I want to play in that research game Dr. Martin has just talked about, because I don't have much of a stomach for that kind of work. A lot of it, in spite of what Dr. Martin has said, does seem to carry a certain feel of futility.

However, I would like to talk of one thing that just came to my mind, and it is something that we have not touched upon yet in the conversation. That is the valuation of water companies for property tax purposes. Most taxing jurisdictions levy against investor-owned companies that provide water service to cities or other jurisdictions, and these companies operate as public utilities. Their valuation might lend itself to a certain amount of systematic research, perhaps even more so than some of the things that Dr. Martin just mentioned. One of the things we have noticed in some preliminary work is that when these water companies are sold to a public buyer, they appear to be sold at a higher price than if they were sold to a private buyer. Obviously, a public owner *can* pay more for them because they will now be free of property tax and income tax, but theoretically a public agency *should* not pay more for them than a private bidder because it doesn't have to. Theoretically the public agency would only have to pay $1 more than the highest bidder from the private sector because there is no competition with other public agencies. But my impression is that the public agencies have not been hard bargainers in their acquisitions or the courts have been somewhat more generous when the transfer was made under eminent domain. The research we did in the California State Board of Equalization indicated there was a two-level pricing system on sales of water companies. I would be interested in seeing this matter explored further because there is the view in the California State Equalization Board that water companies that are purchased by public agencies are priced at reproduction cost less depreciation, and by analogy, then, telephone companies and gas companies and electric companies should be appraised at reproduction cost less depreciation. My contention is that you should assess a water company as well as a telephone or a gas and electric company at the price at which it would sell to a taxpaying buyer and not the price which a tax-exempt agency might pay for it. That is all I have to suggest.

Reeves: Dr. Bonbright, what do you have to add in the way of areas of research?

Bonbright: Because of my interest in pure valuation theory, I would suggest a study aimed at getting toward a rational basis for apportionment of the value of an interstate unit among states and also among local taxing jurisdictions. What is a reasonable basis of apportionment in view of the fact that, except in rare cases, it is not possible to assign to each part an amount equal to the actual value of that part. The value of the New Jersey portion of the interstate railroad is almost zero if you are considering what it could be sold for separately on the open market. On the other hand, what the New Jersey portion is worth to the whole railroad may not be much less than the entire railroad is worth. Yet neither value can serve as a fair basis of apportionment. The assessor should therefore attempt only to get a reasonable apportionment of the total value without any pretense that what he is after is this will-of-the-wisp of finding out the real value or the market value or any other value, strictly defined. I would suggest therefore, that the research be undertaken to determine a more desirable basis for apportionment, not beclouded by the false assumption that what you are trying to find out is value.

Martin: I think that assumption is much less frequent now than it used to be. I think we have already been getting away from it or have got away from it. We say among ourselves here that we allocate a fair share of the unit value to a state and let it go at that. There is misunderstanding to the contrary, but there have been some cases in fairly recent years—one back in the 1950s, for instance, that goes right along with that particular doctrine. So this is a problem that even a lawyer can see through eventually after a long time.

Welch: The Western States Association of Tax Administrators attempted to standardize the allocation of various public utilities by publishing a committee report in 1971, although to the best of my knowledge the report's recommendations are not adhered to in all states at all times.

McCreath: I think we all need to take another look at those recommendations and try to find out why they have not been adopted by the various western states. We have started first with airlines, which we are now reviewing. Isn't the easy answer to why they are not adhered to at least in the case of railroad property the perpetual argument between bridge states and terminal states? I don't think you will ever overcome that particular problem. We are attempting to do that right now with airlines, and Vic Bredehoft of Oregon is heading up a committee that has had about four meetings in the past two months working to solve that problem for airlines anyway.

McSwain: Ron, you asked how much it is being used. I had an occasion to make a study in which I contacted every state, and I found that only two or three were actually employing the formula recommended in that Western States Tax Administrators' publication.

Welch: You are not talking about the 1949 report of the NATA Committee on Railroad Allocation?

McSwain: No. I am talking about the Western States and the report of 1971.

Welch: I think the same might hold for the NATA railroad formula. There might have been one or two states that at one time were using it.

McSwain: We used it at one time, and we threw it out. I think there are not over two states using it now. Very few states use either the NATA or the Western States formula for allocation. Maybe that kind of points up the hopelessness of the whole task.

Morrison: Just a quick question on your water company comment, Ron. It sounds to me as if some of the public buyers did not apply their own appraisal talents on those particular purchases if your two-tier price theory is correct. If there is a higher price level when the buyer is a public entity, would that not violate the definition of willing buyer/willing seller that is essential to market value transactions? If there is only one buyer in the market, does that really constitute an arm's-length transaction between willing buyers and willing sellers?

Welch: I don't think the absence of competition on the buyer's side makes it inadmissible as evidence of value as long as the seller is willing to sell at that price and that the purchaser was willing to buy at that price. Of course, there may be a threat of condemnation that would make it a forced sale. Usually, the condemnation threat has the opposite effect and knocks the price down rather than enhancing the price.

McSwain: Sometimes when you are spending public money, the public officials feel they do not have to get a return on their investment, so they might not bargain as hard as a purchaser who was buying to make a profit on his investment. Public money gets spent more freely than private money.

Welch: But they really can make money for the community on the investment. They can afford to pay more than the private buyer can afford to pay, and they can also reduce the water rates to the consumers because they do not have to pay any taxes of any kind. So what may be an excessive price in the sense that it exceeds the private owner's withholding price can look like a very good buy and very likely is a good buy for the community.

Reeves: They are not buying the same thing as a private purchaser would be buying. The rules have changed.

Fleming: Regulation might also be involved. You are taking it out from under regulation, and it might have a different value when it is not regulated than when it is.

Harriss: I would like to raise a question. Do state officials who are valuing public service corporation property for tax purposes need data to do their job that they are not getting now?

Welch: They sure do in the case of railroads. The income accounts of railroads do not lend themselves to appraisal work. You have to take a lot on faith or else fly in the face of accepted appraisal principles because you really don't know what is in the reported income of the railroad.

Harriss: Why is that? Because they expense their capital improvements?

McSwain: Yes, and because they can juggle their figures. One year when they have a very good income, they can spend a great deal on maintenance. Next year the income may be down and they want their statement to look good, so they cut out some of the maintenance, and then their income will be higher.

Martin: That is one of the reasons that some of us in the case of railroads and other utility property have been in favor of using income averaging. Even though we say we do not believe in it, we find we must use it anyhow. This is much more largely dictated by railroad practice than by the other public service corporations. But it is not absent from the others.

Reeves: I think it is time now to turn to Seth Franzman for a summary of everything we had said here.

Franzman: I recognized at the very outset yesterday that it was going to be impossible to summarize a conversation of this type! However, I do have a few observations that I would like to relate. I think that in our conversation over the last two days we have raised more questions than we have answered, and I think that is the mark of a good meeting. If we had gone home with every question answered, then we would never have to meet again, and I don't think that ever happens in the real world. We have been through a process here of sharing ideas, and I think that process is as old as man himself. When man found an easier way to do a job, he shared that information with someone else, and they took that and adapted it to their own uses. We have done that here.

We have found there are many ideas that need further exploration, and there will be other opportunities in the future to share information. We hope we can find better solutions to these problems we face. I have heard it expressed many times yesterday and today without hesitation, without reluctance, that I do not know. This in my opinion is the mark of maturity. We are able to recognize and admit that we do not know the answers to a lot of these questions. It is doubly reassuring to hear outstanding authorities such as Bonbright, Martin, and Welch make that statement. It is reassuring to know that the people who are the recognized leaders in the evaluation field have areas in which they are uncertain. So we do know that all the problems are not solved.

I think it is important to go back to page 1 of Bonbright's two volumes, which states that the first step in the appraisal process is to determine the purpose of the appraisal. This in itself indicates that there are different values for different purposes in appraising the same property. This is a recognition that we need to make and one to which Coleman Coffey alluded earlier. It is also important to reiterate Dr. Martin's statement that we should undertake research even though we do not expect to find the answer because we can learn as much from our failures as from our successes. If we only undertook work in which we were certain of success, a lot of good work would never get done. Columbus and other explorers operated on that basis, and they have been moderately successful.

Appendixes

Appendix A:
Comments on Bonbright's
Valuation of Property

It would be safe to state that the two volumes on *The Valuation of Property* authored by James C. Bonbright and published in 1937 (The Michie Company, Charlottesville, N.C.) are the most widely quoted reference works on valuation ever published. The subtitle "A Treatise on the Appraisal of Property for Different Legal Purposes" explains the multipurpose function of this two-volume classic in the field of valuation.

Volume I deals with the concepts of value, methods of valuation, and valuation for specific legal purposes. Volume II treats tax valuations under the unit rule from the standpoint of its historical development and then moves on to legal and economic analyses of this important concept in ad valorem tax administration. While Volume II may not contain as much information of interest to the property tax administrator as Volume I, it does contain an excellent chapter on valuation for public utility rate-making purposes. Its concluding chapter underscores the significance of the statement that *"value* is a word of many meanings."

Appendix B:
Valuation Issues Decided
by the Oregon Tax Court

Throughout the conversations, Don Fisher of Oregon makes references to the handling of numerous items of valuation that came into question in the Oregon Tax Court in the case of *Pacific Power and Light Company v. Department of Revenue, State of Oregon*. Many of these items came into sharper focus when Judge Carlisle B. Roberts of the Oregon Tax Court handed down his decision on the tenth of October 1977. Cases No. 987 and 1095 were consolidated for trial since both suits involved common questions of law and fact. Judge Roberts' findings generally were adverse to the position taken by the appraisers in the Oregon Department of Revenue.

Pacific Power and Light challenged the Oregon Department of Revenue's appraisal for ad valorem tax purposes on the following counts:

The department added to the indicated system value by the income approach estimates of the present value of deferred federal income taxes.

The department included in its market data approach (stock and debt) the value of a portion of deferred federal income taxes.

The department added materials and supplies to the stock-and-debt indicator of value.

The department was in error in estimating future operating income.

The department was in error in using a 9 percent rate of capitalization.

The department erred in using a weighted average of the cost income and market approaches to arrive at a final estimate of value.

The Department of Revenue's appraiser testified that he used only the income approach in arriving at his final value estimate. In ruling against the department on this count, Judge Roberts said: "The court agrees with the plaintiff that all three approaches to value should have been used in these cases and that the witness for the defendant having adverted to each approach was in error in not utilizing all of them since each would contribute to the validity of the final result."

The Department of Revenue's appraiser testified that he used the annuity method of capitalization, a method in which (a) there is no requirement that the depreciation be reinvested in order to keep the income stream level, and (b) the depreciation component or return of invested capital is assumed to be immediately reinvested at the assumed rate of return of the original investment.

In ruling against the Department on this count, Judge Roberts stated: "The court agrees with plaintiff that the defendant's annuity method of capitalization and the rates used for sinking fund purposes were in error in these suits and should not be utilized in determining the property values for the subject property in the subject years."

The court did not lay down any hard and fast rules on the handling of depreciation expense. However, the court did state: "Regulatory requirements are legal conditions which must be fully recognized by potential sellers and buyers and consequently by appraisers wherever they have an impact on value."

Judge Roberts also took exception to the Department of Revenue's use of performance ratios to project future income to be capitalized in the income approach. The wording of Judge Roberts' opinion lends tacit approval to the method of estimating future income by "least-squares" trendlines.

In the handling of construction work in progress, the court indicated that this item is reflected in the stock-and-debt approach without adjustment and that knowledgeable buyers would take a conservative approach when estimating present worth of future income to be produced from construction work in progress.

Since the conversations on valuation had such frequent reference to the handling of deferred federal income taxes in the valuation process, it seems wise to quote Judge Roberts' complete statement on this item:

Plaintiff cites as a principal error Mr. Arrowsmith (the Oregon Department of Revenue appraiser) use and treatment of "deferred taxes." After determining a system value for the plaintiff's subject property, he proceeded to derive an additional value for plant "built with deferred taxes," as part of his income approach. . . . This is an extremely important and technical issue in the present suits. Useful background for an understanding thereof can be obtained by reading *Appalachian Power Company v. Federal Power Commission.* . . . Mr. Arrowsmith's treatment of the deferred taxes was in compliance with an order of his supervisor, Victor N. Bredehoeft, based upon a study by Mr. Bredehoeft, set out in plaintiff's exhibit 6, amended by plaintiff's exhibit 7. The study does not carry conviction to the court. This is an instance where, for purposes of valuation of a public utility property, the requirement of ad valorem taxation must be distinguished from valuation-for-rate-regulation purposes. The regulated treatment of "deferred taxes," arising from the allowable federal income tax treatment under IRC (1954) Chapter 167 and former Chapter 168, should be replaced, using instead the treatment ordinarily given to income taxes for those are necessarily involved in the approaches to the valuation of property for ad valorem taxation. Any values growing out of "deferred taxes" for property tax purposes will be reflected in the cost approach (HCLD) and in the stock-and-debt approach. They are a deductible expense as reported in the income approach.

The plaintiff also questioned the income to be capitalized in the income approach. The department used a figure of $157,529,700 compared to

$88,031,000 actually earned by Pacific Power and Light Company during the 1975 assessment year. In handling this question, the court said:

In using the income approach, the appraiser is concerned with the present worth of the future benefits of a property. This is generally measured by the net income *which a fully informed person is warranted in assuming* the property will produce during its remaining useful life. . . . In applying this standard rule, the words "fully informed" and "warranted," in this paragraph, must be given their usual meaning. The appraiser's own judgment is on trial here. Certainly, appraisers should avoid the casual use of speculative future income. . . . The appraiser must place himself in the position of a knowledgeable buyer who is investing his resources and obligating himself to repay money loaned him for the purpose of purchasing the property. The reasonable, prudent person, as purchaser, will strongly discount future speculative income for purposes of capitalization. . . . It was the duty of the defendant's appraiser to test his results for the reasonableness of what he had done. . . . An acceptable appraisal would not have varied so grossly from the plaintiff's actual earnings in the 1975 assessment year.

The Department of Revenue used capitalization rates of 9.0 percent for 1975 and 9.5 percent for 1976. These rates were based upon *a moving five-year average of annual capitalization rates*. Judge Roberts goes on to say:

Such an average inevitably results in the minimizing of the capitalizing rate and the maximizing of income, producing an inflated valuation. . . . As the defendent admitted in its exhibit E, 14: "It should be kept in mind that the so-called current cost of money is the target. . . ." As the plaintiff has concluded in its opening briefs, 54: "If the Department had correctly employed Mr. Fisher's (its administrator) band-of-investment method, it should have developed cap rates of 13.18 percent and 12.43 percent respectively for the years 1975 and 1976 (plaintiff's exhibit 25)."

However, as applied to these particular suits, the court is in agreement with the plaintiff that the most appropriate cap rates would be not less than the rates of 13.13 percent for 1974 and 12.29 percent for 1975. . . . Defendant in its answering brief, 38, ET SEQ., argues that it is the long-term view that the department takes in selecting cap rates. . . . However, no authority is cited for its stand. . . . To the court there appears to be no justification for the department's rationale; i.e., that the department has historically followed a practice of changing capitalization rates slowly to reflect long-term changes in the cost of capital and that the interest rates that existed in 1974 and 1975 were not typical.

Judge Roberts' decision is accompanied by extensive quotations from appraisal literature, and it would be read with interest by anyone involved in the market value appraisal of utility property for ad valorem tax purposes.

Appendix C:
"Oregon Court Holds Power Company's Nuclear Fuel Is Not Inventory"

The Property Taxes section of the September 1977 issue of *Tax Administrators News* carried the following item:

OREGON COURT HOLDS POWER COMPANY'S NUCLEAR FUEL IS NOT INVENTORY

The Oregon Tax Court has held that a power company's store of nuclear fuel for use in an electric generating plant did not constitute inventory for purposes of property tax assessment. The court also ruled that plans and specifications being prepared for the power company by an out-of-state firm were not "work in progress" taxable to the power company as personal property with situs in Oregon.

The taxpayer was an Oregon power company. The state argued that its store of nuclear fuel for conversion into electricity was not inventory, which is assessable at a lower rate. The court agreed, rejecting the taxpayer's argument that the fuel fit the statutory definition of inventory as materials that are or will become part of the stock in trade of the taxpayer. The company contended that its stock in trade was energy, which was stored in fuel and from which it "flowed," rather than being manufactured or produced. The court ruled that it was not the intent of the legislature to include such items within its definition.

In the matter of the plans and specifications, the court found that the work was owned by the engineering firm which was preparing it, and would not be delivered to the taxpayer until completion. Although the taxpayer had made large cash advances to the engineers, this gave it no property rights in the work itself. The court ruled that the right to receive created by the payments could not be considered to be held by the taxpayer in its business or to have a situs in Oregon. It held that it could not have been the intent of the legislature to tax such an executory contract.

Note: *Portland General Electric Company v. Department* was decided March 1, 1977.

Appendix D:
Public Law 94-210—What the Act Is and What It Says

Section 306 of Public Law 94-210, titled The Railroad Revitalization and Regulatory Reform Act, has as its stated objective prohibiting discriminatory tax treatment of railroad transportation property. It states that transportation property shall not be assessed at a higher ratio to market value than all other commercial and industrial property in the same assessment jurisdiction and that no other discriminatory tax shall be imposed on such property. Disputes involving this matter come under the jurisdiction of the district courts of the United States. The provisions of this section shall not become effective until three years after the date of its enactment, which was February 5, 1976.

In order for transportation properties to obtain relief, the ratio of assessment value to market value of transportation property must be at least 5 percent in excess of the ratio for all other commercial and industrial property in the same assessment jurisdiction. The ratio of assessed value to market value of all other commercial and industrial property shall be determined by a random sampling method known as a sales assessment ratio study. If this ratio cannot be established to the satisfaction of the court, then it will use a sales ratio based on all other property assessed for taxation in the jurisdiction (basically residential and farm properties). Unfortunately, at the present time assessment ratios for commercial and industrial property are seldom available.

143

Appendix E:
Society Creates Value,
Court Rules in Landmark
Railway Terminal Case

Economic value is one thing, but there is also a value created by and returnable to the public, the New York State Court of Appeals has ruled in a case that may have broad significance in the appraisal of landmark buildings.

The case arose when the bankrupt Penn Central railroad wanted to use one of its assets, Grand Central Station in New York City, to get out of some of its economic problems. An office tower was planned using air rights above the terminal. However, the city then designated the station a landmark, which precluded the development as Penn Central had planned.

Thus arose the issue of whether the company was being deprived of its right to earn a "fair return" on its property, when the court determined the terminal's value derived not solely from Penn Central's investment, but from government and society's contributions as well. In an opinion written by Chief Judge Charles D. Breitel, this reasoning was stated as follows:

It may be true that no property has economic value in the absence of the society around it, but how much more true it is of a railroad terminal set amid a metropolitan population and entirely dependent on heavy traffic of travelers to make an economically feasible operation. Without people, Grand Central would never have been a successful railroad terminal, and without the terminal, a major transportation center, the proposed building site would be much less desirable for an office building.

Of course it may be argued that had Grand Central never been built, the area would not have developed as it has. Thus, the argument runs, construction of the terminal triggered growth of the area and created much of the terminal property's current value. Indeed, the argument has some validity. But, in reality, it is of little moment which comes first, the terminal or the travelers. For it is the interaction of economic influences—the terminal initially drawing people to the area and the society developing the area with shops, hotels, office buildings and unmatched civil services—that has made the property so valuable. Neither factor alone accounts for the increase in the property's value; both, in tandem, have contributed to the increase.

Of primary significance, however, is that society as an organized entity, especially through its government rather than as a mere conglomerate of individuals, has created much of the value of the terminal property. . . . Railroads have always been a franchised and regulated public utility, favored monopolies at public expense, subsidized and with limited powers of eminent domain without which their existence and character would not have been possible. . . .

A fair return is to be accorded the owner, but society is to receive its due for its share in the making of a once-great railroad. The historical, cultural and architectural resource that remains was neither created solely by the private owner nor solely by the society in which it was permitted to evolve.

About the Editor

Arlo Woolery is executive director of the Lincoln Institute of Land Policy in Cambridge, Massachusetts. Prior to joining the Lincoln Institute in 1975, Mr. Woolery was director of the Arizona State Department of Property Valuation, a post which he held since that department was established in 1967. Before assuming responsibility for the Arizona State Property Tax program, he held several executive positions in radio and television broadcasting and cable television operation and equipment manufacturing. Mr. Woolery has worked closely with the International Association of Assessing Officers and served as a member of that organization's education committee for five years. He has been awarded the designation Certified Assessment Evaluator and is currently a senior instructor in the educational programs of the association. He also serves on the faculty of the Wichita State University program on railroad and utility valuations and is a member of the NTA/TIA Taxation of Public Utilities-Transportation Committee.